THE PLEASURE GROUND

Also by Richard Murphy

POETRY

The Archaeology of Love
('The Dolmen Press, Ireland, 1955)

The Last Galway Hooker
(The Dolmen Press, Ireland, 1961)

Sailing to an Island
(Faber and Faber, UK, 1963)

The Battle of Aughrim and *The God Who Eats Corn*
(Faber and Faber, UK; Alfred A. Knopf, USA, 1968)

High Island
(Faber and Faber, UK, 1974)

High Island: New and Selected Poems
(Harper & Row, USA, 1975)

Selected Poems
(Faber and Faber, UK, 1979)

The Price of Stone
(Faber and Faber, UK, 1985)

The Price of Stone & Earlier Poems
(Wake Forest University Press, USA, 1985)

New Selected Poems
(Faber and Faber, UK, 1989)

The Mirror Wall
(Bloodaxe Books, UK; Wolfhound Press, Ireland;
Wake Forest University Press, USA, 1989)

Collected Poems
(The Gallery Press, Ireland, 2000;
Wake Forest University Press, USA, 2001)

PROSE

The Kick: A Memoir; later *The Kick: A Life Among Writers*
(Granta Books, UK, 2002, 2003; Lilliput Press ebook, 2013)

RICHARD MURPHY

The Pleasure Ground

POEMS 1952-2012

BLOODAXE BOOKS

Copyright © Theodora Lee and Caspar Lee 2013

ISBN: 978 1 85224 986 1

First published 2013 in the UK by
Bloodaxe Books Ltd,
Highgreen,
Tarset,
Northumberland NE48 1RP
and by Lilliput Press
in Ireland.

www.bloodaxebooks.com
For further information about Bloodaxe titles
please visit our website or write to
the above address for a catalogue

Cover design: Neil Astley & Pamela Robertson-Pearce.

Printed in Great Britain by
Bell & Bain Limited, Glasgow, Scotland.

For my daughter Emily
and her husband James Riordan
and my grandchildren
Theodora and Caspar Lee

'The only end of writing is to enable the readers better to enjoy life, or better to endure it.'

SAMUEL JOHNSON

ACKNOWLEDGEMENTS

Dennis O'Driscoll (1954-2012) was the poet, critic, mentor and friend, who, for the past thirty-six years, most generously encouraged and improved my poetry. Poem by poem his warmly critical and intuitive response would guide me to find a better word or a line or an image. His kindness, wit and courtesy made it easy to accept his disapproval. His help was crucial to my completing *The Price of Stone*, a sequence of 50 sonnets written in 1981-1983 and later dedicated to Dennis. *The Pleasure Ground: Poems 1952-2012* is the last achievement of his guidance and friendship.

I thank Barbara Browning Brown, Professor Emeritus of West Virginia University, for her devoted, scrupulous and invaluable help day after day with my writing of prose and poetry during the past sixteen years.

Fifty years ago Thomas Kinsella, over lunch in a Dublin café, advised me to shorten the narrative of 'The Cleggan Disaster'. I put off taking that advice until last year, when Bernard O'Donoghue helped me with his own advice on the revision. I thank them both, and Bernard for allowing his essay on 'Pat Cloherty's Version of *The Maisie*' to be reprinted in this book. The essay first appeared under Peter Denman's guest editorship of 'Poems that Matter: 1950-2000' in the *Irish University Review*, Volume 39 No 2 Autumn/Winter 2009.

I acknowledge with gratitude the support of the Arts Council of Ireland since Aosdána was established in 1982.

Ever since Alan Jenkins became Poetry Editor of the *TLS* he has published many of my best poems. I'm grateful for his long lasting support.

I thank Peter Fallon for publishing my *Collected Poems* at the Gallery Press in Ireland in 2000; and I wish to thank Eiléan Ní Chuilleanáin for publishing 'Waking from a Dream' in *Poetry Ireland Review* 93. It's too late to thank, but I remember with gratitude, three editors who published four of my latest poems: Caroline Walsh, for 'A River of Notebooks' in *The Irish Times*; Barbara Epstein, for 'Rite of Passage' in *The New York Review of Books*; and Mick Imlah, for 'Vagrant' and 'Last Word' in the *TLS*.

The drawing on page 17 is by Ruth Brandt (1936-1989) from *The Last Galway Hooker* (The Dolmen Press, 1961); the one on page 175 is by Patrick Scott from *The Price of Stone*.

Wegiriya, Sri Lanka, 12 February 2013

CONTENTS

PART FOUR

Care and poems of 1974–1984

PART FIVE

The Price of Stone: a sequence of 50 sonnets 1981-1984

PART SIX

Sri Lanka and poems finished the years 1985-2012

THE PLEASURE GROUND

Once, as a child playing in our Pleasure Ground, I swallowed what I thought was a poisonous berry. It fell into my mouth as I watched Mary, my older sister, climbing among the dark green leaves and bright red berries on the overhanging branches of our favourite yew. I rushed indoors to gargle and spit and try to make myself vomit by sticking two fingers down my throat. The fear of dying tortured me. First an hour anxiously passed, then a day, restoring my hope and joy, as the menace of the yewberry passed.

When I was much younger in Ceylon, cobras and vipers lurked in the drains of our garden and every drop of drinking water had to be filtered and boiled. Our Nanny had induced in me a terror of being poisoned. Now we were in holy Ireland, free of snakes and malarial mosquitoes, but liable to die young of incurable diseases called lockjaw, consumption, diphtheria and infantile paralysis. I believed my best chance of living without grievous pain till the age of 21 lay in the strength of my prayers.

I was then about twelve, staying for short holidays with our mother at Milford, her father's old demesne house in south County Mayo. For ten months of the year my elder brother Chris and I were boarding at the Cathedral Choir School in Canterbury. We seldom saw our father, a senior civil servant in the crown colony of Ceylon, which would become Sri Lanka long after independence. Our branch of the family occupied the East Wing of the house, formerly the servants' quarters, converted in 1935 for us to occupy with our mother at our father's expense. Neither he nor his Murphy forbears had ever owned a house or an acre of land.

We loved our Pleasure Ground. A great grey limestone wall wreathed in ivy surrounded it on three sides, enclosing us with midges and horse-flies in a seedy paradise of impoverished Anglo-Irish pride. More than a hundred years ago, we heard, there had been a Lovers' Walk behind a yew hedge above a terrace of roses at the top, but all we could find was an endless thicket of briars and snowberries. Below the terrace stood two sentinel cedars of Lebanon, much too tall to climb, planted by the 'General' who had lost his life fighting Napoleon in Spain. Our grandmother had seen his ghost in uniform standing on the croquet lawn in moonlight. The calls of invisible wood pigeons haunted a copper beech that canopied the lawn.

One day, struggling through hogweed in an orchard just outside the

Pleasure Ground, I came across a very old fig tree, and searching under its big green leaves I found a number of small hard unripe figs. After this, the fig tree was mine. I dug, weeded, manured and sowed seeds in the ground beside it, growing Canterbury bells and sweet peas for my mother's vases; carrots, parsnips, onions, lettuce and cress for us to eat. That became part of my 'war effort' against de Valera's neutrality. We ate what I grew with no fear of being poisoned.

It was the happiest time of my life. Looking out on the Pleasure Ground or sitting under the copper beech, we studied Xenophon and Virgil or Shakespeare and William Blake with two retired teachers who loved poetry. For a whole year we couldn't be sent to schools in England because 'the war was on' and U-boats were sinking passenger ships around Ireland. Instead of work being an imposition, it had here become a delight because it earned my mother's praise.

Everyone was a bit afraid of Grandfather, with his short grey neatly combed hair, his black clothes, his high (meaning Low Church) dog collar, and his monocle hanging by a cord on his chest. He occupied the West Wing, built in William and Mary style shortly after the battles of Aughrim and the Boyne. His study smelt of musty books. I was more intrigued by his three damascened double-barrelled twelve-bore hammer guns by Evans, which he kept in a locked glass cabinet, than by Blackstone's *Commentaries* or Gibbon's *Decline and Fall*. As a clergyman he was in touch with God, but as a retired Lieutenant-Colonel D.S.O. his temper was politely called 'peppery'.

I liked to pause on his staircase to gaze at some early Victorian prints of ancient temples and pagodas in Rangoon. My favourite showed a horde of half-naked Burmese swordsmen climbing over a bamboo stockade defended by a few redcoats with muskets. Amidst the carnage a ferocious native with a curved sword aimed at the neck of a British grenadier is about to be skewered by his bayonet.

Our grandmother in the West Wing never minded what we did, and the worse it was the more she laughed. Here I had been born in the guest room with a swarm of bees in the roof. Granny was always our ally in trouble, sickness or romance. Here my sister was promised her future husband at cards; here ghosts were real because Granny frequently saw them; here were secret chambers she helped us to find, perhaps we'd find a blunderbuss hidden in a time of outrage. There was a tiny graveyard in her garden where her favourite black Labradors were buried, one with the name Annie Snipe carved on a tombstone. Moss roses grew by her well. She told me that sniffing them would help me to fall in love. In her glass-house she kept my orange tree alive.

I'd often find her with medicines and bandages spread in a muddle among the saucepans on her kitchen table, relieving the pain and injuries of children whose parents could not afford to take them to a doctor. The nearest lived in Hollymount, six miles away, on foot or bicycle or horse-drawn side-car. Near and far from Milford she was known as 'the healer'.

Lucy, which I never dreamt of calling her, had been brought up in the house built in 1835 by her Scottish grandfather, General Thomson of the 74th Highlanders, on the dark side of a purple mountain in the picturesque wilderness of Salruck overlooking the Little Killary harbour. That was fifty miles away on the Connemara coast, and we used to motor there in Martin Walsh's Ford V8 from Kilmaine on birthdays and other family occasions. Mary used to bring her painting things, and, seen through our mother's and grandmother's artistic eyes, this land of the dead which we entered, stark, desolate, uncultivated, storm-bound and profoundly mournful, appealed to me romantically more than the nurtured garden of civility we had left.

It was a poor and miserable part of the country. Huddled among rocks, under thatch held down by fishnets tied to stones, were those whose ancestors had lost the struggle for the land which ours had won. The planters of our Pleasure Ground had acquired an estate of 70,000 acres, which famine, revolution and land reform had cut to 350. But these people lived on five or only two-and-a-half-acre holdings. Rocks, rivers, waterfalls, heavy rain, storms at sea, hunger on land, hardship I never suffered, had made them strong and proud. Their manners were rougher than ours, and their Irish songs had tones that clashed with our Anglican cathedral harmonies. I wished I could talk like them. The old people had all the time in the world to tell stories. It was the antidote my fear of death by poison in the Pleasure Ground needed.

Twice before, much earlier in my life, as far back as I can remember, we had lived in Connemara, first by a lake, and later by the sea, that greatest of all pleasure grounds. The house by the lake at Ard-na-Silla had a garden with a deep well into which as a three-year-old I fell while playing with my older brother Chris. On walks along a crooked lane to fetch milk in pails from Miss Welby's cottage, we ate the wild strawberries we picked on the roadside – a delicious treat soured by my fear of swallowing by mistake a poisonous berry such as deadly nightshade.

Our Pleasure Ground period didn't last. Some of us went back to boarding schools in England, others settled abroad. Soon our grandmother was left alone in the big empty house, where we stayed for short holidays. Her mind wandered. The copper beech was cut for firewood to keep her warm. Chickens fouled the beds of our mother's lupins, and rabbits burrowed into our tennis court. When rust unhinged an iron gate, an errant cow ate a mouthful of yew leaves and died.

The yew still bore a crop of berries, the fig tree survived, but the planted symmetry of our Pleasure Ground had vanished. The aura I had breathed under the yew, the fig and the copper beech had gone, the aura that had made poetry, music and painting, even mathematics, an effortless delight. There was no young energy with a will and money to mend walls, plant trees, sow and cultivate and labour. I felt guilty and lost.

So I went back to that older earlier unfenced romantic pleasure ground in the treeless hills of Connemara on the edge of the sea. There, aged nineteen, I abandoned myself to mountains, lakes and waterfalls; stretched without clothes on the ground on summer nights; and once in winter rolled naked in snow. I wanted to write poetry, and believed that someday, like the ripening of the figs, I might taste the fruit and it would not be poisonous. I didn't imagine it would take so long and be so difficult to produce a first crop or a last. As I grew older the Pleasure Ground sank through decay into oblivion, as the old people died and the young left the country. So I searched for grounds of pleasure that excluded nobody, till I found them by living with friends I loved among people on or near the sea. There I tried to write poetry true to that life in words put together to last.

And now, aged 84, living on rice and curry in the hinterland of Sri Lanka, facing paddy fields between wooded hills crowned by Buddhist temples, while keeping connected through the Internet, I remember with gratitude all the friends, fellow poets, relations , editors, publishers and readers in Ireland, England and America, who have helped and inspired me to write.

January 31, 2012
Wegiriya, Sri Lanka

PART ONE

Sailing to an Island
and poems of the years
1952-1962

Sailing to an Island

The boom above my knees lifts, and the boat
Drops, and the surge departs, departs, my cheek
Kissed and rejected, kissed, as the gaff sways
A tangent, cuts the infinite sky to red
Maps, and the mast draws eight and eight across
Measureless blue, the boatmen sing or sleep.

We point all day for our chosen island,
Clare, with its crags purpled by legend:
There under castles the hot O'Malleys,
Daughters of Granuaile, the pirate queen
Who boarded a Turk with a blunderbuss,
Comb red hair and assemble cattle.
Across the shelved Atlantic groundswell
Plumbed by the sun's kingfisher rod,
We sail to locate in sea, earth and stone
The myth of a shrewd and brutal swordswoman
Who piously endowed an abbey.
Seven hours we try against wind and tide,
Tack and return, making no headway.
The north wind sticks like a gag in our teeth.

Encased in a mirage, steam on the water,
Loosely we coast where hideous rocks jag,
An acropolis of cormorants, an extinct
Volcano where spiders spin, a purgatory
Guarded by hags and bristled with breakers.

The breeze as we plunge slowly stiffens:
There are hills of sea between us and land,
Between our hopes and the island harbour.
A child vomits. The boat veers and bucks.
There is no refuge on the gannet's cliff.

We are far, far out: the hull is rotten,
The spars are splitting, the rigging is frayed,
And our helmsman laughs uncautiously.
What of those who must earn their living
On the ribald face of a mad mistress?
We in holiday fashion know
This is the boat that belched its crew
Dead on the shingle in the Cleggan disaster.

Now she dips, and the sail hits the water.
She luffs to a squall; is struck; and shudders.
Someone is shouting. The boom, weak as scissors,
Has snapped. The boatman is praying.
Orders thunder and canvas cannonades.
She smothers in spray. We still have a mast;
The oar makes a boom. I am told to cut
Cords out of fishing-lines, fasten the jib.
Ropes lash my cheeks. Ease! Ease at last:
She swings to leeward, we can safely run.
Washed over rails our Clare Island dreams,
With storm behind us we straddle the wakeful
Waters that draw us headfast to Inishbofin.

The bows rock as she overtakes the surge.
We neither sleep nor sing nor talk,
But look to the land where the men are mowing.
What will the islanders think of our folly?

A whispering spontaneous reception committee
Nods and smokes by the calm jetty.
Am I jealous of these courteous fishermen
Who hand us ashore, for knowing the sea
Intimately, for respecting the storm
That took nine of their men on one bad night
And five from Rossadillisk in this very boat?

Their harbour is sheltered. They are slow to tell
The story again. There is local pride
In their home-built ships.
We are advised to return next day by the mail.

But tonight we stay, drinking with people
Happy in the monotony of boats,
Bringing their catch to the Cleggan market,
Cultivating fields, or retiring from America
With enough to soak till morning or old age.

The bench below my knees lifts, and the floor
Drops, and the words depart, depart, with faces
Blurred by the smoke. An old man grips my arm,
His shot eyes twitch, quietly dissatisfied.
He has lost his watch, an American gold
From Boston gasworks. He treats the company
To the secretive surge, the sea of his sadness.
I slip outside, fall among stones and nettles,
Crackling dry twigs on an elder tree,
While an accordion drones above the hill.

Later, I reach a room, where the moon stares
Through a cobwebbed window. The tide has ebbed,
Boats are careened in the harbour. Here is a bed.

Wittgenstein and the Birds

A solitary invalid in a fuchsia garden
Where time's rain eroded the root since Eden,
He became for a tenebrous epoch the stone.

Here wisdom surrendered the don's gown
Choosing, for Cambridge, two deck chairs,
A kitchen table, undiluted sun.

He clipped with February shears the dead
Metaphysical foliage. Old, in fieldfares
Fantasies rebelled though annihilated.

He was haunted by gulls beyond omega shade,
His nerve tormented by terrified knots
In pin-feathered flesh. But all folly repeats

Is worth one snared robin his fingers untied.
He broke prisons, beginning with words,
And at last tamed, by talking, wild birds.

Through accident of place, now by belief
I follow his love which bird-handled thoughts
To grasp growth's terror or death's leaf.

He last on this savage promontory shored
His logical weapon. Genius stirred
A soaring intolerance to teach a blackbird.

So before alpha you may still hear sing
In the leaf-dark dusk some descended young
Who exalt the evening to a wordless song.

His wisdom widens: he becomes worlds
Where thoughts are wings. But at Rosroe hordes
Of village cats have massacred his birds.

1953

Girl at the Seaside

I lean on a lighthouse rock
Where the sea-gowns flow,
A trawler slips from the dock
Sailing years ago.

Wine, tobacco and seamen
Cloud the green air,
A head of snakes in the rain
Talks away desire.

A sailor kisses me
Tasting of mackerel,
I analyse misery
Till Mass bells peal.

I wait for clogs on the cobbles,
Dead feet at night,
Only a tempest blows
Darkness on sea-light.

I've argued myself here
To the blue cliff-tops:
I'll drop through the sea-air
Till everything stops.

St Guenolé, December 1954

The Archaeology of Love

You have netted this night
From the sea a vase
Which once we carried
At the festivals
In Phaestos where
A young prince ruled
And a stone leopard
Crouched on the walls
Guarding those granaries
And the golden bulls.

Until one April hour's
Earthquake of defeat
By galleys that grooved
Our unwary waters,
When the oil of peace
Blazed in every cruse,
Home became for us
The weltering sea
And language a hiss
In the wood of oars.

Through gorges on the run
Alone I crawled
To a scorpion plain
Dry with poppies
To bury the stolen
Treasure of cities,
And I passed those years
Dumb below pines
A slave to the pleasures
Of the land of quince.

By the nets of your grace
My heart was hauled
Out of heavy mud,
And tonight we sailed
To this island garden
Flaming with asphodel,
Moonlight raking
The early corn,
While the spades rang
On our lost foundation.

I have learnt to restore
From dust each room
An earthquake lowered
In that doomed spring,
To piece beyond the fire
A cypress court
With gryphons basking,
Wander in the snow
Of almonds before
Those petals were wasting.

You have taken this night
Years of grievance
From my silted heart
And broken the script
Into household language;
You have cut into me
A gypsum field
Happy with harvesters
Fluting the sky
With sheaves on their shoulders.

Phaestos, February 1955
with Patricia Avis

To a Cretan Monk in Thanks for a Flask of Wine

God bless you Dionysus
For your wedding gift of wine
Poured from a ten-year cask
With prayers to make children
Where hyacinths and anemones
Flower on a terraced hill.

In the black robes of a monk
With a Byzantine beard
You decant us a drink
Laughing like a goatherd
On a mountain with his flock
Giving us a cup of ecstasy.

Ageing at your monastery
With rifles in your cell
Smelling of cedar and rosemary
Sombrely you recall
The German occupation
And the paratroops you shot.

God bless you Dionysus
Now your nectar has propelled
Our bodies to create
Concord, works of art,
Our wedded lives like melting
Snow, unfolding a green world.

Rethymnon, 1955
with Patricia Avis

Auction

When furniture is moved
From a dead-free home
Through lean, loved
Rooms alone I come,

To bid for damp etchings,
My grandaunt's chair,
Drawers where rings
Of ruby in water flare.

A sacked gardener
Shows me yew hedges
House high, where
The dead made marriages.

With what shall I buy
From time's auctioneers
This old property
Before it disappears?

Epitaph on a Douglas Fir

She grew ninety years through sombre winter,
Rhododendron summer of midges and rain,
In a beech-wood scarred by the auctioneer,

Till a March evening, the garden work done,
It seemed her long life had been completed,
No further growth, no gaiety could remain.

At a wedding breakfast bridesmaids planted
With trowel and gloves this imported fir.
How soon, measured by trees, the party ended.

Arbour and crinoline have gone under
The laurel, gazebos under the yews:
Wood for wood, we have little to compare.

We think no more of granite steps and pews,
Or an officer patched with a crude trepan
Who fought in Rangoon for these quiet acres.

Axes and saws now convert the evergreen
Imperial shadows into red deal boards,
And let the sun enter our house again.

Quickly we'll spend the rings that she hoarded
In her gross girth. The evening is ours.
Those delicate girls who earthed her up are faded.

Except for daffodils, the ground is bare:
We two are left. They walked through pergolas
And planted well, so that we might do better.

Lake Park, Roundwood, 1956

The Woman of the House

In memory of my grandmother Lucy Mary Ormsby
of Milford, Kilmaine, County Mayo, 1873-1958

On a patrician evening in Ireland
I was born in the guest room: she delivered me.
May I deliver her from the cold hand
Where now she lies, with a brief elegy?

It was her house where we spent holidays,
With candles to bed, and ghostly stories:
In the lake of her heart we were islands
Where the wild asses galloped in the wind.

Her mind was a vague and log-warmed yarn
Spun between sleep and acts of kindliness:
She fed our feelings as dew feeds the grass
On April nights, and our mornings were green.

In those happy days, when in spite of rain
We'd motor west where salmon boats tossed,
She would sketch on the pier among the pots
Waves in a sunset, or the rising moon.

Indian-meal porridge and brown soda-bread,
Boiled eggs and buttermilk, honey from gorse,
Far more than we wanted she always offered
In a heart-surfeit: she ate little herself.

Mistress of mossy acres and unpaid rent,
She crossed the walls on foot to feed the sick:
Though frugal cousins frowned on all she spent
People had faith in her healing talent.

She bandaged the wounds that poverty caused
In the house that famine labourers built,
Gave her hands to cure impossible wrong
In a useless way, and was loved for it.

Hers were the fruits of a family tree:
A china clock, the Church's calendar,
Gardeners polite, governesses plenty,
And incomes waiting to be married for.

How the feckless fun would flicker her face
Reading our future by cards at the fire:
Rings and elopements, love letters, old lace,
A signet of jokes to seal our desire.

'It was sad about Maud, poor Maud!' she'd sigh
To think of the friend she lured and teased
Till she married the butler. 'Starved to death,
No service either by padre or priest.'

Cholera raged in the Residency:
'They kept my uncle alive on port.'
Which saved him to slaughter a few sepoys
And retire to Galway in search of sport.

The pistol that lost an ancestor's duel,
The hoof of the horse that carried him home
To be stretched on chairs in the drawing-room,
Hung by the Rangoon prints and the Crimean medal.

Lever and Lover, Somerville and Ross
Have fed the same worm as Blackstone and Gibbon,
The mildew has spotted *Clarissa*'s spine
And soiled the *Despatches of Wellington*.

Beside her bed lay an old Bible that
Her Colonel Rector husband used to read,
And a new *Writers' and Artists' Yearbook*
To bring a never printed girlhood back.

The undeveloped thoughts died in her head,
But from her heart, through the people she loved
Images spread, and intuitions lived,
More than the mere sense of what she said.

At last, her warmth made ashes of the trees
Ancestors planted, and she was removed
To hospital to die there, certified.
Her house, but not her kindness, has found heirs.

Compulsory comforts penned her limping soul:
With all she uttered they smiled and agreed.
When she summoned the chauffeur, no one obeyed,
But a chrome hearse was ready for nightfall.

'Order the car for nine o'clock tonight!
I must get back, get back. They're expecting me.
I'll bring the spiced beef and the nuts and fruit.
Come home and I'll brew you lime flower tea!

'The house in flames and nothing is insured!
Send for the doctor, let the horses go.
The dogs are barking again. Has the cow
Calved in the night? What is that great singed bird?

'I don't know who you are, but you've kind eyes.
My children are abroad and I'm alone.
They left me in this jail. You all tell lies.
You're not my people. My people have gone.'

Now she's spent everything: the golden waste
Is washed away, silent her heart's hammer.
The children overseas no longer need her,
They are like after-grass to her harvest.

People she loved were those who worked the land
Whom the land held in chains of poverty.
They've gone; a tractor ploughs where horses strained;
Some roofless houses hold their history.

Through our inheritance all things have come,
The form, the means, all by our family:
The good of being alive was given through them,
We ourselves limit that legacy.

The bards in their beds once beat out ballads
Under leaky thatch listening to sea birds,
But she in the long ascendancy of rain
Served biscuits on a tray with ginger wine.

Time can never relax like this again:
She on a side-car with her sketch-book,
He writing a sermon in the library
Till lunch, then fishing all the afternoon.

On a wet winter evening in Ireland
I let go her hand, and we buried her
In the family earth beside her husband.
Only to think of her, now warms my mind.

1958

Droit de Seigneur

1820

In a grey rectory a clergyman was reading
Fortunate by firelight the *Connaught Journal.*
The shutters were closed, for famine was spreading
Among the people. A portrait of Cromwell,
One hand on the Bible, the other on a sword,
Had been stowed that evening under a haystack.
The air was crackling with the whips of rhetoric.

A groom was saddling his mare in the stable
While a redcoat stumbled down the loft ladder
Buttoning his tunic, followed by a girl
Who ran to the kitchen. The yard lantern
Yellowed the stirrups and the buckled leather
On the mare's girth as he combed her down.
The master was for hunting the Ribbonmen:

A secret band swearing oaths by moonlight,
Refusing to pay tithes or rent to the landlord,
Who battered on lonely doors after midnight
And kept in their pockets a green ribbon.
He called it his duty to commit these rogues
To the jury of gentlemen at Galway Assizes.
Saving of property went with saving of souls.

So he galloped out with a few soldiers
On to the gravelled road under the lime trees
With his father's pistol in a handsome holster.
They ambushed a wedding from the next parish.
All escaped except a young simpleton
On whom they found a scrap of green cloth.
Twenty miles to Galway he was marched in chains.

In the pigeon park the heifers were grazing
Under the beech trees. The soldiers had gone.
Behind the frown of the windows, browsing
On the price of cattle in the *Connaught Journal*,
The rector looked out on the frost and the sun.
The girl ran across the yard with a bucket.
'Tomorrow,' he read, 'the boy will be executed.'

Grounds

You were not there. I don't know who
That morning lit your cigarette:
But I was there because of you
To take the consequence of deceit
Asking a man in a wig, who'd not
Known or loved you, to interfere
Between us and our daughter.

Four years ago a civil farce
Was paid for, and they dragged in God,
Contracts, champagne, telegrams, cars:
But now needless pomp had dwindled
To needless echoes – 'Yes, m'Lud,'
'No, m'Lud' – and I had lost you,
Lost everything we had gone through.

In white letters on black paper
A judge decreed we were dissolved
From all the good we owed each other,
From all the bad left unresolved.
What we were hangs dead in the air
As dust from a second-hand book
Picked off a shelf and put back.

In a dream you appear to me – sick
And lost in rain on a high cliff
Crying and careless where you walk.
A lighthouse flashes far, far off:
But I cannot, though I try to, speak
To stop the harm in all I've done
Dragging you down and down.

London, 1959

The Last Galway Hooker

Where the Corrib river chops through the Claddagh
To sink in the tide-race its rattling chain
The boatwright's hammer chipped across the water

Ribbing this hooker, while a reckless gun
Shook the limestone quay-wall, after the Treaty
Had brought civil war to this fisherman's town.

That 'tasty' carpenter from Connemara, Cloherty,
Helped by his daughter, had half-planked the hull
In his eightieth year, when at work he died,

And she did the fastening, and caulked her well,
The last boat completed with old Galway lines.
Several seasons at the drift-nets she paid

In those boom years, working by night in channels
With trammel and spillet and an island crew,
Tea stew on turf in the smoke-filled forecastle,

Songs of disasters wailed on the quay
When the tilt of the water heaved the whole shore.
'She was lucky always, the *Ave Maria*',

With her brown sails, and her sleek skin of tar,
Her forest of oak ribs and larch-wood planks,
Cut limestone ballast, costly fishing gear,

Fastest in the race to the gull-marked banks,
What harbour she anchored in, there she was queen
Her crew could afford to stand strangers drinks,

Till the buyers failed in nineteen twenty-nine,
When the cheapest of fish could find no market,
Dumped overboard, the price down to nothing;

Until to her leisure a fisher priest walked
By the hungry dockside, full of her name,
Who made a cash offer, and the owners took it.

Then like a girl given money and a home
With no work but pleasure for her man to perform
She changed into white sails, her hold made room

For hammocks and kettles, the touch and perfume
Of priestly hands. So now she's a yacht
With pitch-pine spars and Italian hemp ropes,

Smooth-running ash-blocks expensively bought
From chandlers in Dublin, two men get jobs
Copper-painting her keel and linseeding her throat,

While at weekends, nephews and nieces in mobs
Go sailing on picnics to the hermit islands,
Come home euphoric having hooked a few dabs.

*

Munich, submarines, and the war's demands
Of workers to feed invaded that party
Like fumes of the diesel the dope of her sails,

When the priest was moved inland to Athenry
From the stone and reed patches of lobstermen
Having sold her to Michael Schofield P.C.,

Best among the boatmen of Inishbofin,
She his best buy. He shortened the mast, installed
An 'Ailsa Craig' engine, made a hold of her cabin,

Poured over the deck tar and pitch slightly boiled;
Every fortnight he drained the sump in the bilge
'To preserve the timbers'. All she could do, fulfilled.

The sea, good to gamblers, let him indulge
His fear when she rose winding her green shawl
And his pride when she lay calm under his pillage:

And he never married, was this hooker's lover,
Always ill-at-ease in houses or on hills,
Waiting for weather, or mending broken trawls:

Bothered by women no more than by the moon,
Not concerned with money beyond the bare need,
His joy was to sleep in her forepeak cabin.

A neap-tide of work, then a spring of liquor
Were the tides that alternately pulled his soul,
Now on a pitching deck with nets to hand-haul,

Then passing Sunday propped against a barrel
Winding among words like a sly helmsman
Till stories gathered around him in a shoal.

She was Latin blessed, holy water shaken
From a small whiskey bottle by a surpliced priest,
Madonnas wafered on every bulkhead,

Oil-grimed by the diesel, and her luck lasted
Those twenty-one years of skill buoyed by prayers,
Strength he inherited from sea-going ancestors.

She made him money and again he lost it
In the fisherman's fiction of turning farmer:
The cost of timber and engine spares increased,

Till a phantom hurt him, ribs on a shore,
A hulk each tide rattles that will never fish,
Sunk back in the sand, a story finished.

*

We met here last summer, nineteen fifty-nine,
Far from the missiles, the moon-shots, the money,
And we drank looking out on the island quay,

While his crew were abroad building a motorway.
Old age had smoothed his barnacled will:
With a farewell song he sold me the *Ave Maria*.

Then he was alone, stunned like a widower –
Relics and rowlocks pronging from the wall,
A pot of boiling garments, winter everywhere,

Especially in his bones, watching things fall,
Hooks of three-mile spillets, trammels at the foot
Of the unused double bed – his mind threaded with all

The marline of his days twined within that boat,
His muscles' own shackles then staying the storm
Which now snap to bits like frayed thread.

*

So I chose to renew her, to rebuild, to prolong
For a while the spliced yards of yesterday.
Carpenters were enrolled, the ballast and the dung

Of cattle he'd carried lifted from the hold,
The engine removed, and the stale bilge scoured.
De Valera's daughter hoisted the Irish flag

At her freshly adzed mast this Shrove Tuesday,
Stepped while afloat between the tackle of the *Topaz*
And the *St John*, by Bofin's best boatmen,

All old as himself. Her East End sail maker,
West Quarter boatwright, Cloonamore helmsman
Picked up the tools of their ancestral craft,

And in memory's hands this hooker was restored.
Old men my instructors, and with all new gear
May I handle her well down tomorrow's sea-road.

Inishbofin, 1960

The Drowning of a Novice

At Easter he came
   with a March wind blowing,
A lapsed Benedictine
   whose mind was fabling

An island where the monks
   like cormorants
Fished from the rocks
   in black garments.

He thought he could quietly
   with his own boat
Be fed by the sea;
   and with a spade

In winter find cockles
   and clams to eat.
But for her novice
   the sea grew white

Flowers in her garden
   petalled with spray.
He had brought no chart
   and he lost his way.

Where was the pebbled cove
   and the famine cottage?
His piano-playing fingers
   ached at the oars.

Book-disputes that he dreaded
   reared up in waves,
His catechised head
   was coldly doused.

Now his feet were washed
   in the sluicing bilges.
For his last swim
   there were no prizes.

When his dinghy went down
   at a sheer shore
And the swell slogging,
   his arms opened

As if to his mother,
   and he drowned.
An island beachcomber
   Picked up an oar.

Theodore Roethke at Inishbofin, 1960

On a wet night, laden with books for luggage,
And stumbling under the burden of himself,
He reached the pier, looking for a refuge.

Darkly he crossed to the island six miles off:
The engine pulsed, the sails invented rhythm,
While the sea expanded and the rain drummed softly.

Safety on water, he rocked with a new theme,
While a poem in his mind's greenhouse bloomed
On the model of a Saginaw chrysanthemum.

The deep trough of his depression was becalmed
In the womb of the harbour. Lyrics came in a trance.
To be loved by the people, he, a stranger, hummed

In the herring store on Sunday crammed with drunks
Ballads of bawdry with a speakeasy stress.
Yet lonely they left him, 'one of the Yanks'.

The children understood. This was not madness.
How many orphans had he fathered in words
Robust and cunning, but never heartless.

He watched the harbour scouted by sea birds:
His fate was like fish under poetry's beaks:
Words began weirdly to take off inwards.

Time that they calendar in seasons not in clocks,
In gardens dug over and houses roofed,
Was to him a see-saw of joys and shocks,

Where his body withered but his style improved.
A storm shot up, his glass cracked in a gale:
An abstract thunder of darkness deafened

The listeners he'd once given roses, now hail.
He'd burst the lyric barrier: logic ended.
Doctors were called, and he agreed to sail.

Travelling Player

At evening time
From cocks of hay
Children come
To a green marquee
Pitched at the dock
Where trawlers lie
To hear the clack
Of a dancer's shoes
And watch the trick
Of a conjuror's nose.

She sang as a child
With Marie Lloyd,
Ran wild
On the caravan road.
Now she is old
Her silks are soiled
There are holes in her shoes
And she feels a fake
While every night
She marries the duke.

She does not play
Her life story,
She tries to tease
With a tinsel fan,
An opera hat
And a silver cane –
'I'm Burlington Bertie
I rise at ten-thirty' –
While the summer rain
Seeps through the tent.

In a caravan fire
Her children were burnt.
Now all the lighter
Her merriment
On the creaking stage
To hide her rage.
Dance and deceive,
O dance and live!
While the haymakers sleep
She drowses on dope.

Connemara Marble

The cut is cooled by water
Douched where the discs revolve
To the drum of a far off motor
Slicing the polished cliff,
While under the shapeless mountain
Marble masons ponder
Souvenirs in the chunks of stone.

That gritty green-gashed line!
Why whorl it with charm
Into ashtrays and shamrocks,
Round towers, Celtic crosses?
Old men who wind the crane
Seem careless of the harm
Done to the quarried stone.

The marble of mackerel wanes
In sun on a hooker's deck,
But in shops this marble shines
Or swings from a girl's neck:
Why do the makers falter
And carve a weaker shape
Than a fish iced on a slab?

The Cleggan Disaster

off the west coast of Ireland in 1927

Five boats were shooting their nets in the bay
After dark. It was cold and late October.
The hulls hissed and rolled on the sea's black hearth
In the shadow of stacks close to Inishbofin.
Rain drenched the rowers with no drying wind.
From the strokes of the oars a green fire flaked
And briskly quenched. The shore-lights were markers
Easterly shining across the Blind Sound.

Five pieces of drift-net with a mesh of diamonds
Were paid from each stern. The webbed curtains hung
Straight from the cork-lines, and warps were hitched
To the strong stems and the pine oars boarded.
The men in the boats lit their pipes and rested.

The flood-tide fell slack, all the breakers calmed.
Not a flicker of a fish, only the slow fall
Of the ocean drawing out the last drops of sleep.
Soon they could feel the current of the ebb
Tugging their nets, lifting the mooring-stones
Off the sandy bottom. Two boats began to haul.

From the bows of a boat in the centre of the bay
Concannon watched and waited. On each side
He heard them hauling. He held the guide rope
Attached to the cork-line, so he could feel
If a shoal struck the nets. But so far, nothing.

Why had those others hauled? They were old
Experienced boatsmen. A man on the East End
Quay had warned him, 'Sharpen your knife,
Be ready for trouble, cut away your nets.
Your crew is too young.' Were they going home?

The night looked fair enough for them to fill
Barrels with salted fish to last the winter.

He had respect for the sea, he gave away
A share of his catch at the Cleggan market,
No one who asked for a feed of fish was refused.
On Bofin Island he loafed on the land,
Dozed through dreary winters dreaming of boats
And in summer wanted neither food nor sleep
While he gave the sea all his strength of mind.

He was sure of his boat, built on the island
With Cong Forest timber, oak, elm and larch;
Long supple pine oars, thole-pins of holly
And a grapnel forged by the Cleggan smith.
She'd always been lucky, never lost a man.

He was doubtful of his crew, three men and a boy
Who needed the money. Their land was poor
And they had no heart for this work on water.
They had to fish or go hungry half the year
With so many children at home to be fed.
That night the best of boatsmen were on the bay
And many who wished they'd waited by the fire.

In the dark before the moon rose, he could smell
Fish-oil and blood oozing from the nets
Where a shark was gorging on the tails of mackerel.
So he hauled until he reached the snarled threshes
Of the coiled shark, which he stunned across the rail
And clubbed with a foot-stick bursting its blood.

Shouts of joy clanged around the horseshoe bay
As luck began to load the boats with fish
While a shoal of mackerel in his chain of nets
Glimmered across his rail, jetting green fire
In the black brazier of the rolling bilges.

Having three more pieces of net to haul
Concannon thought, 'If we're too greedy
We could sink the boat. We've caught enough
To reach home safely, thanks be to God.
Cut the nets now and haul them tomorrow.
Darker it's getting and the wind's rising.'

The night was like a shell, with long sea surges
Loudening from afar, making them all afraid.
Quickly they folded the nets and heaped the fish.
The moon was kindling, the sky smouldering,
Mackerel flapped in the bilge. A woman was calling,
Crying from the beach. A shiver rippled the spine
Of the stony headland. Then, on the glistening gong
Of the sleeping sea, a terrible storm struck.
None of the boats could reach the nearby shore.

The men began to pray. Stack-funnelled hail
Crackled in volleys, with blasts on the bows
Where Concannon stood to fend with his body
The slash of seas. Then sickness surged,
And against their will they were griped with terror.
He told them to bail. When they lost the bailer
They bailed with their boots, casting overboard
Two costly nets with a thousand mackerel.

She was drifting down the sound, her mooring-stone lifted
By the fingers of the tide plucking at the nets
Which he held with burning hands. Over and over
He heard in his heart, 'Keep her stem to the storm,
And the nets will help her to ride the water:
Meet the force of the seas with her bows,
Each wave as it comes.' Later he'd use the knife.

Down in the deep where the storm could not go
The strong ebb-tide was drawing to windward
Their cork-buoyed ninety-six fathom of nets
With thousands of mackerel thickly meshed,

Tugging the boat off rocks on the mainland shore.
The moon couldn't shine, the clouds shut her out,
But she came unseen to sway on his side
All the waters gathered from the great spring tide.

As he slid from the cliff-slope of a heaped wave
Down the white and violet skin of turbulence
Into the boiling trough, he gathered in
Loose hanks of net, until the scalding rope
Steamed from his hands, the brittle boat, convulsed
By the far crest, shot through the spindrift safe.

The oarsmen were calling Concannon to let go,
Take it easy for a while. Let the boat drift
To the Cleggan shore, downwind, till they touch land.
Even there, if they died, it would be in a bay
Fringed with friends' houses, instead of in the open
Ocean, where the lost would never be found,
Where nobody is buried, no prayers are said.
Concannon silenced them, and stiffened his hold.

Twice the lightning blinked, then a crash of thunder.
Three cliffs of waves collapsed above them, seas
Crushed in his face, he fell down, and was dazed.

The wind began to play, like country fiddlers
In a crowded room with nailed boots stamping
On a stone cottage floor, raising white ashes.
The sea became a dance. He staggered to the floor
As the music unleashed him, spun in a circle.
Now he was dancing the siege of Death:
Now he was Death, they were dancing around him,
White robed dancers with crowns and clubs,
With white masked faces, and hands like claws
Flaying his eyes, as they clinched and swung.
He was holding the rope as the dance subsided.

While he lay there stunned, he remembered the sea
In tar-melting sunlight, dry weed on the thwarts,
The gills of mackerel tight in the meshes,
Hot stench of dead fish in the bilges,
Planks gaping wide and thole-pins screeching,
Long fishing-lines grooving the gunwales,
His hands hauling up the apostle's John Dory.
He would never say, like that cripple on the quay,
He wished he had not wasted his life on the sea.

He knelt against the stem, his palms bleeding,
His eyes, dimmed by the scurf of salt,
Straining to give shape to the shadows they saw
That looked like men in the milder water.
One of the crew said he heard his brother
Shouting for help, two oars away;
Yet when he hollered, there was no reply.
In a flash of lightning, a white hand rose
And rested on the gunwale, then slowly sank.

Down the valleys of this lull, like a black cow
In search of her calf, an upturned hull
Wallowed towards them. Her stem had parted.
All hands must have been lost. She lunged to his side
And almost staved him. Were the men inside?
Those who had thrown him his ropes from the quay?
The one who had warned him about his crew?
No help for them now. With his foot on her planks
He fended her off. As she bore away,
Her keel like a scythe cut a clear white swath
Through the gale's acres. Then a great sea crossed.

What were those lights that seemed to blaze like red
Fires in the pits of waves, lifted and hurled
At the aching sockets of his eyes, coals that lit
And expired in the space of a swell's slow heave?
'Am I going blind? Those waves look like rocks.

Now *there's* a light. Count the seconds…a slow pulse.
I can see that light from my own back door,
Slyne Head, never so high, such piercing brightness.
Where has it gone? Was it south of us it shone?'

Lights flickered and vanished. Like a grey seal
Blinded by shot, he clung to the stem, his eyes closed.
The boy shouted, 'There's rocks to leeward.'
'What rocks do you think?' another asked.
'Dog Rock, I think, I fished here last summer.'
Concannon drew his knife: 'I'm cutting the nets.'
Piece by piece he slashed, but he had to tear
The clinging hanks with his finger bones, at last
He severed the guide rope that had saved them
And sank to his knees. The oarsmen rowed,
Backwards, falling away, her bows facing the storm,
With their eyes fixed on the faint lamps
That led across calm waters to Cleggan Quay.

It was three o'clock when she nudged the steps.
Safe on the stone bollards they fastened their ropes.
The full moon was whitening the ribs of hulks
In the worm-dark dock. The tide was flowing
As they trudged to the village, his crew his guide:
The sea had not claimed him, she had left him blind.

Lanterns shone from the gates of the fish-store
Freshly that night cleaned for a *céilí*.
Bodies of fishermen lay on the floor on boxes,
Blood on their faces. Five had been found
By troops of searchers on shingle and sand.
Over the bier, with one hand cupping a flame,
An old man was looking at his drowned son.

As the day dawned, news spread of the lost.
Michael O'Toole's boat, wrecked on Letter beach,
Had floated off on the morning tide:

Only his body was got, the skull fractured:
He had crawled above high water mark and died.
From the village of Rossadillisk they lost sixteen,
Nine from Inishbofin, and more from Inishkea.
The walking stick of a man who was lame
Was found in a heap of kelp on a silver strand.
There was a king of the Mayo fishermen
Drawn from the sea chained in his own nets.
Of those who survived, a young one was seen
Walking at noon on a hill, clutching a bailer.

YEARS LATER

Whose is that hulk on the shingle
The boatwright's son repairs
Though she has not been fishing
For thirty-four years
Since she rode the disaster?
The oars were turned into rafters
For a roof stripped by a gale.
Moss has grown on her keel.

Where are the red-haired women
Chattering along the piers
Who gutted millions of mackerel
And baited the spillet hooks
With mussels and lugworms?
All the hurtful hours
Thinking the boats were coming
They hold against those years.

Where are the barefoot children
With brown toes in the ashes
Who went to the well for water,
Picked winkles on the beach

And gathered sea-rods in winter?
The lime is green on the stone
Which they once kept whitewashed.
In summer nettles return.

Where are the dances in houses
With porter and cakes in the room,
The reddled faces of fiddlers
Sawing out jigs and reels,
The flickering eyes of neighbours?
The thatch which was neatly bordered
By a fringe of sea-stones
Has now caved in.

Why does she stand at the curtains
Combing her seal-grey hair
And uttering bitter opinions
On hungry soil and woeful sea,
Drownings and famines?
When will her son say,
'Forget about the disaster,
We're mounting nets today!'

PART TWO

The Battle of Aughrim 1691

and

The God Who Eats Corn 1963

THE BATTLE OF AUGHRIM, 1691

A meditation on colonial war and its consequence in Ireland
written in Connemara between 1962 and 1967.

I NOW

On Battle Hill

Who owns the land where musket-balls are buried
In blackthorn roots on the esker, the drained bogs
Where sheep browse, and credal war miscarried?
Names in the rival churches are written on plaques.

Behind the dog-rose ditch, defended with pikes,
A tractor sprays a rood of flowering potatoes:
Morning fog is lifting, and summer hikers
Bathe in a stream passed by cavalry traitors.

A Celtic cross by the road commemorates no battle
But someone killed in a car, Minister of Agriculture.
Dairy lorries on the fast trunk-route rattle:
A girl cycles along the lane to meet her lover.

Flies gyrate in their galaxy above my horse's head
As he ambles and shies close to the National School –
Bullets under glass, Patrick Sarsfield *Would to God...* –
And jolts me bareback on the road for Battle Hill:

Where a farmer with a tinker woman hired to stoop
Is thinning turnips by hand, while giant earth-movers
Shovel and claw a highway over the rector's glebe:
Starlings worm the aftergrass, a barley crop silvers,

And a rook tied by the leg to scare flocks of birds
Croaks as I dismount at the death-cairn of St Ruth:
Le jour est a nous, mes enfants, his last words:
A cannonball beheaded him, and sowed a myth.

Green Martyrs

I dream of a headless man
Sitting on a charger, chiselled stone.

A woman is reading from an old lesson:
'…who died in the famine.

'Royal bulls on my land,
I starved to feed the absentee with rent.

'Aughrim's great disaster
Made him two hundred years my penal master.

'Rapparees, whiteboys, volunteers, ribbonmen,
Where have they gone?

'Coerced into exile, scattered
Leaving a burnt gable and a field of ragwort.'

July the Twelfth, she takes up tongs
To strike me for a crop of calf-bound wrongs.

Her weekly half-crowns have built
A grey cathedral on the old gaol wall.

She brings me from Knock shrine
John Kennedy's head on a china dish.

Orange March

In bowler hats and Sunday suits,
Orange sashes, polished boots,
Atavistic trainbands come
To blow the fife and beat the drum.

Apprentices uplift their banner
True blue dyed with 'No Surrender!'
Claiming Aughrim as if they'd won
Last year, not 1691.

On Belfast silk, Victoria gives
Bibles to kneeling Zulu chiefs.
Read the moral, note the date:
'The secret that made Britain great.'

Derry, oakwood of bright angels,
Londonderry, dingy walls
Chalked at night with *Fuck the Queen*
Bygone canon, bygone spleen.

Casement's Funeral

After the noose, and the black diary deeds
Gossiped, his fame roots in prison lime:
The hanged bones burn, a revolution seeds.
Now Casement's skeleton is flying home.

A gun salutes, the troops slow-march, our new
Nation atones for her shawled motherland
Whose welcome gaoled him when a U-boat threw
This rebel quixote soaked on Banna Strand.

Soldiers in green guard the draped catafalque
With chalk remains of once ambiguous bone
Which fathered nothing till the traitor's dock
Hurt him to tower in legend like Wolfe Tone.

From gaol yard to the Liberator's tomb
Pillared in frost, they carry the freed ash,
Transmuted relic of a death-cell flame
Which purged from martyrdom the diarist's flesh.

On the small screen I watch the packed cortège
Pace from High Mass. Rebels in silk hats now
Exploit the grave with an old comrade's speech:
White hair tossed, a black cape flecked with snow.

Historical Society

I drive to a symposium
 On Ireland's Jacobite war,
Our new élite in a barrack-room
 Tasting vintage terror.

Once an imperial garrison
 Drank here to a king:
Today's toast is republican,
 We sing 'A Soldier's Song'.

One hands me a dinted musket-ball
 Heated by his palm.
'I found this bullet at Aughrim
 Lodged in a skull.'

Slate

Slate I picked from a nettle-bed
Had history, my neighbour said.

To quarry it, men had to row
Five miles, twelve centuries ago.

An inch thick, it hung watertight
Over monks' litany by candlelight:

Till stormed by viking raids, it slipped.
Four hundred years overlapped.

Pirates found it and roofed a fort
A mile west, commanding the port.

Red-clawed choughs perched on it saw
Guards throw priests to the sea's jaw.

Through centuries of penal gale
Hedge scholars huddled where it fell.

Pegged above a sea-wormed rafter
It rattled over landlord's laughter.

Windy decades pined across
Barrack roof, rebellion, moss.

This week I paved my garden path
With slate St Colman nailed on lath.

Inheritance

Left a Cromwellian demesne
My kinsman has bulldozed three bronze age raths.

No tree can survive his chainsaw:
Hewing is part of the land reclamation scheme.

He has auctioned grandfather's Gallipoli sword
And bought a milking machine.

Slate he stripped from a Church of Ireland steeple
Has broadened his pigsty roof:

Better a goat's hoof in the aisle
Than rosary beads or electric guitars.

Five hundred cars pass the stone lion gates
For a civil war veteran's funeral.

On a grave behind a petrol pump
The wind wraps a newspaper around an obelisk.

On ancient battleground neat painted signs
Announce 'Gouldings Grows'.

Christening in Kilmaine, 1927

A side-car creaks on the gravel drive,
The quality arrive.

With Jordan water
They mean to give me a Christian start.

Harmonium pedals squeak and fart.
I'm three weeks old.

It's a garrison world:
The good are born into the Irish gentry.

What do they hope my use of life will be?
Duty.

Fight the good fight:
Though out of tune, if loud enough, it's right.

Under the Holy Table there's a horse's skull
Shot for a landlord's funeral:

From a religious duel
The horse cantered the wounded master home.

Two clergy christen me: I'm saved from Rome.
The deaf one has not heard my name,

He thinks I am a girl.
The other bellows: 'It's a boy, you fool!'

History

One morning of arrested growth
An army list roll-called the sound
Of perished names, but I found no breath
In dog-eared inventories of death.

Touch unearths military history.
Sifting clay on a mound, I find
Bones and bullets fingering my mind:
The past is happening today.

The battle cause, a hand grenade
Lobbed in a playground, the king's viciousness
With slaves succumbing to his rod and kiss,
Has a beginning in my blood.

II BEFORE

Legend

The story I have to tell
Was told me by a teacher
Who read it in a poem
Written in a dying language.
Two hundred and fifty years ago
The poet recalled
Meeting a soldier who had heard
From veterans of the war
The story I have to tell.

Deep red bogs divided
Aughrim, the horse's ridge
Of garland hedgerows and the summer dance,
Ireland's defence
From the colonists' advance:
Twenty thousand soldiers on each side,
Between them a morass
Of godly bigotry and pride of race,
With a causeway two abreast could cross.

In opposite camps our ancestors
Ten marriages ago,
Caught in a feud of absent kings
Who used war like a basset table
Gambling to settle verbal things,
Decide if bread be God
Or God a parable,
Lit matches, foddered horses, thirsted, marched,
Halted, and marched to battle.

St Ruth's Address to the Irish Army

'Gentlemen and Fellow Souldiers,' said the Marquis of St Ruth, addressing the Irish army with a speech translated into English, which was found on the body of a slain Irish officer and quoted by the Reverend George Story in *An Impartial History of the Wars of Ireland*:

'I Suppose it is not unknown to you, and the whole Christian World, what Glory I have acquired, and how Successful and Fortunate I have been in Suppressing Heresie in France, and propagating the Holy Catholick Faith, and can without Vanity boast my Self the happy Instrument of bringing over thousands of poor deluded Souls from their Errours, who owe their Salvation to the pious care of my thrice Illustrious Master, and my own Industry, assisted by some holy Members of our unspotted Church: while great numbers of those incourigable Hereticks have perished both Soul and Body by their obstinacy.

'It was for this reason that the most Puissant King my Master, Compassionating the miseries of this Kingdom, hath chosen me before so many worthy Generals to come hither, not doubting but by my wonted Diligence I should Establish the Church in this Nation, on such a foundation as it should not be in the power of Hell or Hereticks hereafter to disturb it: And for the bringing about of this Great and Glorious Work, next the Assistance of Heaven, the unresistable Puisance of the King my Master, and my own Conduct; the great dependance of all good Catholicks is on your Courage.

'I must confess since my coming amongst you, things have not answered my wishes, but they are still in a posture to be retrieved, if you will not betray your Religion and Countrey, by an unseasonable Pusilanimity.

'I'm assured by my Spyes, that the Prince of Oranges Heretical Army, are resolved to give us Battle, and you see them even before you ready to perform it. It is now therefore, if ever that you must indeavour to recover your lost Honour, Priviledges and Forefathers Estates: You are not Mercinary Souldiers, you

71

do not fight for your Pay, but for your Lives, your Wives, your Children, your Liberties, your Country, your Estates; and to restore the most Pious of Kings to his Throne: But above all for the propagation of the Holy Faith, and the subversion of Heresie. Stand to it therefore my Dears, and bear no longer the Reproaches of the Hereticks, who Brand you with Cowardise, and you may be assured that King James will Love and Reward you: Louis the Great will protect you; all good Catholicks will applaud you; I my self will Command you; the Church will pray for you, your Posterity will bless you; Saints and Angels will Caress you; God will make you all Saints, and his holy Mother will lay you in her Bosome.'

A Wife's Complaint

Teigue in his green coat rides to war,
Nuts are swelling in the hazel wood.
My father's ten black heifers low,
I've lost the father of my unborn child.

Last night he left me in a copse weeping
When foragers bugled there'd be a battle.
Proudly he gallops in Sarsfield's troop,
My tongue less to him than a drum's rattle.

Martial Law

A country woman and a country man
Come to a well with pitchers,
The well that has given them water since they were children:
And there they meet soldiers.

Suspecting they've come to poison the spring
The soldiers decide to deal
Justly:
So they hang them on a tree by the well.

The Sheepfold

On Kelly's land at Aughrim, all is the same
As the old people remember, and pray it will be,
Where his father grazed sheep, like all before him.

Mullen the herd, propped by a fallen tree,
His mouth scabbed and his cheeks pitted by pox,
Blows on a reed pipe a sad melody.

Ripe seeds are bending the tall meadow stalks.
He stops, when the sun sparks on a cuirass...
A goatskin drum across the sheep-walk tucks.

*

Buff-coated horsemen jump the walls, and press
The bleating flock, while Kelly pleads for pay:
'By the Holy Virgin, give us gold, not brass!'

Raw lancers, goading footsore ewes away
With rancid udders drained by thriving lambs,
Say, 'D'you grudge men food who fight for you?'

Soon they reach camp, where flies hover in swarms
On entrails at the bivouacs, and they smoke
The meat on spits, lice crawling in their uniforms.

*

Farmer and herd follow with crook and stick,
Their grey slack tweed coats tied with twists of straw,
Reeking of wool and sour milk and turf smoke,

Uphill through hedge gaps to an ancient rath
Embanked by hawthorn, where the Catholic flag
Blazoned with Bourbon lilies for St Ruth

Floats white and gold above a deep red bog,
And here they halt, blessing themselves, and kneel:
'Christ make the Frenchman pay us for our flock!'

*

Inside, they see a hand with a swan quill
That writes and writes, while powdered clerks translate,
Quoting with foreign voice the general's will:

'Children, I bring from France no better aid
To toast the image-wreckers on hell fire
Than my own skill to lead your just crusade.

'It is your duty, since I wage this war
For your souls' sake, to lose your flock, but win
A victory for your conscience and my honour.'

*

'Give back our fleeces!' begs the shepherd, then
St Ruth's head rises: '*Foutez-moi le camp!*'
Guards clash steel halberds, and the natives run.

Through glacial esker, by the river Suck
They choose the bog path to the richer camp
With tongues to talk and secret prayers for luck.

All day packhorses laden westwards tramp
Trundling bronze cannon behind casks of shot,
While eastwards, armed with spite, two traitors limp.

*

The Danish mercenaries they chance to meet
Standing in hogweed, sheltered by a ditch,
Assume they're spies, with no one to translate,

So fetch them to a grey house, where the Dutch
Commander who serves England's Orange king
Shakes hands, and gives them each a purse to clutch,

While a blond adjutant runs off to bring
The gunner Trench, who'll need their eyes next day,
When the cold cannon mouths start uttering.

Mercenary

They pick us for our looks
To line up with matchlocks,
Face shot like sandbags,
Fall, and manure the grass
Where we wouldn't be let trespass
Alive, but to do their work
Till we dropped in muck.

Who cares which foreign king
Governs, we'll still fork dung,
No one lets *us* grab soil:
Roman or English school
Insists it is God
Who must lighten our burden
Digging someone else's garden.

Dragoon

I share a tent with Dan, smelling of seals
Whose oil he smears on his French matchlock
Drooling idly for hours about camp girls.

Polishing his plug bayonet, he boasts he'll hack
From a shorn heretic a pair of testicles
To hang above St Brigid's Well for luck.

Soft west wind carries our friary bells
Against the tide of psalms flooding the plain.
Now Dan fills a powder-horn, his cheek swells.

'Learn him our creed,' he says, 'garotte your man:
Tomorrow night we'll eat like generals.'
Our supper meat is prodded, sniffed by Dan.

God's Dilemma

God was eaten in secret places among the rocks
His mother stood in a cleft with roses at her feet
And the priests were whipped or hunted like stags

God was spoken to at table with wine and bread
The soul needed no heavenly guide to intercede
And heretics were burnt at stakes for what they said

God was fallen into ruins on the shores of lakes
Peasants went on milking cows or delving dikes
Landlords corresponded with landlords across bogs

Planter

Seven candles in silver sticks,
Water on an oval table,
The painted warts of Cromwell
Framed in a sullen gold.
There was ice on the axe
When it hacked the king's head.
Moths drown in the dripping wax.

Slow sigh of the garden yews
Forty years planted.
May the God of battle
Give us this day our land
And the papists be trampled.
Softly my daughter plays
Sefauchi's Farewell.

Dark night with no moon to guard
Roads from the rapparees,
Food at a famine price,
Cattle raided, corn trod,
And the servants against us
With our own guns and swords.
Stress a hymn to peace.

Quite music and claret cups,
Forty acres of green crops
Keep far from battle
My guest, with a thousand troops
Following his clan call,
Red-mouthed O'Donnell.
I bought him: the traitor sleeps.

To whom will the land belong
This time tomorrow night?
I am loyal to fields I have sown
And the king reason elected:
Not to a wine-blotted birth mark
Of prophecy, but hard work
Deepening the soil for seed.

Rapparees

Out of the earth, out of the air, out of the water
And slinking nearer the fire, in groups they gather:
Once he looked like a bird, but now a beggar.

A fish rainbows out of a pool – 'Give me bread!'
He fins along the lake shore with the starved.
Green eyes glow in the night from clumps of weed.

The water is still. A rock or the nose of an otter
Jars the surface. Whistle of rushes of bird?
It steers to the bank, it lands as a pikeman armed.

With flint and bundles of straw a limestone hall
Is gutted, a noble family charred in its sleep,
And they gloat by moonlight on a mound of rubble.

The highway trees are gibbets where seventeen rot
Who were caught last week in a cattle raid.
The beasts are lowing. 'Listen!' 'Stifle the guard!'

In a pine wood thickness an earthed-over charcoal fire
Forges them guns. They melt lead stripped from a steeple
For ball. At the drumming of a snipe each can disappear

Terrified as a bird trapped in a gorse fire,
To delve like a mole or mingle like a nightjar
Into the earth, into the air, into the water.

III DURING

St Ruth

St Ruth trots on a silver mare
Along the summit of a ridge
Backed by a red cavalcade
Of the King's Life Guards.
He wears a blue silk tunic,
A white lace cravat,
Grey feathers in his hat.

He has made up his mind to put
The kingdom upon a fair combat:
Knowing he cannot justify
Losing Athlone
Before his Most Christian master,
He means to bury his body
In Ireland, or win.

The army commander only speaks
French and Italian:
His officers know English,
Their men only Irish.
When he gives an order
His jowls bleach and blush
Like a turkey-cock's dewlap.

Lieutenant-General Charles Chalmont,
Marquis of St Ruth,
The Prince of Condé's disciple
In the music of war,
Jerks with spinal rapture
When a volley of musket fire
Splits his ear.

Picture his peregrine eyes,
A wife-tormentor's thin
Heraldic mouth, a blue
Stiletto beard on his chin,
And a long forked nose
Acclimatised to the sulphurous
Agony of Huguenots.

He keeps his crab-claw tactics
Copied from classical books
An unbetrayable secret
From his army of Irishmen.
He rides downhill to correct
A numerical mistake
In his plan's translation.

He throws up his hat in the air,
The time is near sunset,
He knows victory is sure,
One cavalry charge will win it.
'*Le jour est à nous, mes enfants,*'
He shouts. The next minute
His head is shot off.

The Winning Shot

Mullen had seen St Ruth riding downhill
And Kelly held a taper. 'There's the Frenchman!'
Trench laid the cannon, a breeze curved the ball.

The victory charge was halted. Life Guards stooped down
And wrapped the dripping head in a blue cloak,
Then wheeled and galloped towards the setting sun.

Chance, skill and treachery all hit the mark
Just when the sun's rod tipped the altar hill:
The soldiers panicked, thinking God had struck.

Patrick Sarsfield

Sarsfield rides a chestnut horse
At the head of his regiment,
His mountainous green shoulders
Tufted with gold braid,
Over his iron skull-piece
He wears the white cockade.
A bagpipe skirls.

Last summer after the Boyne
When King James had run,
He smashed the Dutch usurper's
Waggon-train of cannon
Benighted at Ballyneety.
Patrick Sarsfield, Earl of Lucan
Commands the reserve today.

The saviour of Limerick knows
Nothing of St Ruth's plan,
Not even that the battle
Of Aughrim has begun.
He has obeyed since dawn
The order to wait for further
Orders behind the hill.

He sees men run on the skyline
Throwing away muskets and pikes,
Then horsemen with sabres drawn
Cutting them down.
He hears cries, groans and shrieks.
Nothing he will do, or has done
Can stop this happening.

Men at the Castle

Comely their combat
    amidst death and wounds,
Romantic their disregard
    for material details:
The wrong kegs of ball
    were consigned to the castle,
Irish bullets too large
    for French firelocks.
A great stronghold
    became a weakness.
Till sunset they loaded
    muskets with tunic buttons
To fire on cavalry,
    squadron after squadron
Crossed the causeway
    and flanked their front.
Heroic volleys
    continued until nightfall:
They fell with no quarter
    when the battle was lost.

Henry Luttrell

Luttrell on a black charger
At the rear of his regiment
Stands idle in a bean-field
Protected by a tower.
He wears a dandy yellow coat,
A white-feathered hat
And a gilded sabre.

When he hears the word spread
Along the line, 'St Ruth is dead,'
He retreats at a trot:
Leading his priding cavalry
To betray the humble foot:
Ten miles to a dinner, laid
In a mansion, then to bed.

Prisoner

Night covers the retreat.
Some English troops beating a ditch for loot
Capture a wounded boy. 'Don't shoot!'

'What'll we do with him?'
'I'll work in the camp.' 'Strip him!'
Naked he kneels to them. They light a lamp.

'Pretty boy.' 'Castrate the fucker!'
'Let the papist kiss my flute.'
'Toss a coin for the privilege to bugger…'

He cries like a girl. 'Finish him off.'
'No, keep him alive to be our slave.'
'Shove a sword up his hole.' They laugh.

A tipsy officer calls out:
'You men be on parade at eight.
I want no prisoners, d'you hear me? Shoot

The crowd we took, when it gets light.
We've no more food. Good night.
God knows you all put up a splendid fight.'

IV AFTER

The Wolfhound

A wolfhound sits under a wild ash
Licking the wound in a dead ensign's neck.

When guns cool at night with bugles in fog
She points over the young face.

All her life a boy's pet.
Prisoners are sabred and the dead are stripped.

Her ear pricks like a crimson leaf on snow.
Horse carts creak away.

Vermin by moonlight pick
The tongues and sockets of six thousand skulls.

*

She pines for his horn to blow
To bay in triumph down the track of wolves.

Her forelegs stand like pillars through a siege.
His Toledo sword corrodes.

Nights she lopes to the scrub
And trails back at dawn to guard a skeleton.

Wind shears the berries from the rowan tree,
The wild geese have flown.

She lifts her head to cry
As a woman keens in a famine for her son.

*

A redcoat, stalking, cocks
His flintlock when he hears the wolfhound growl.

Her fur bristles with fear at the new smell,
Snow has betrayed her lair.

'I'll sell you for a packhorse,
You antiquated bigoted papistical bitch!'

She springs. In self-defence he fires his gun.
People remember this.

By turf embers she gives tongue
When choirs are silenced in wood and stone.

The Reverend George Story Concludes
An Impartial History of the Wars in Ireland

I never could learn what became of St Ruth's corpse:
Some say he was left stript amongst the dead,
When our men pursued beyond the hill;
And others that he was thrown into a Bog:
However, though the man had an ill character
As a great persecutor of Protestants in France,
Yet we must allow him to be very brave in his person,
And indeed considerable in his conduct,
Since he brought the Irish to fight a better battle
Than ever that people could boast of before:
The behaved themselves like men of another nation.

But it was always the genius of this people
To rebel, and their vice was laziness.
Since first they began to play their mad pranks
There have died, I say, in this sad kingdom,
By the sword, famine and disease,
At least one hundred thousand young and old.
Last July alone, more execution was done
At Aughrim than in all Europe besides.
Seen from the top of the hill, the unburied dead
Covered four miles, like a great flock of sheep.

What did the mere Irish ever gain
By following their lords into rebellion?
Or what might they have gotten by success
But absolute servitude under France?
They are naturally a lazy crew
And love nothing more than to be left at ease.
Give one a cow and a potato garden
He will aspire to no greater wealth
But loiter on the highway to hear news.

Lacking plain honesty, but most religious,
Not one in twenty works, the jails are full
Of thieves, and beggars howl on every street.
This war has ended happily for us:
The people now must learn to be industrious.

Henry Luttrell's Death

Luttrell, Master of Luttrellstown
Sat in a gold and red sedan
The burden of a hungry urchin
And a weak old man
Barefoot on cobbles in the midnight rain,
Up torch-lit quays from a coffee shop
Where after supper, the silver cup
Lifted, a fop had said,
'It's time to bury Aughrim's dead.'

A poor smell of ordure
Seeped through his embroidered chair,
He slid the glass open for air,
Waved off a beggar groping at the door
And watched six black dray-horses cross
The river. 'Let the traitor pass.'
He felt his pocket full of pebbles
Which he used at Mass in straw-roofed chapels
To lob at little girls.

The chair slewed at his town house,
Flambeaus, footmen in place,
And plunked him down.
He'd sold his country to preserve his class,
The gutters hissed: but that was done
Twenty-six years ago, he said,
Had they not buried Aughrim's dead?
Standing under grey cut stone
A shadow cocked a gun.

No one betrayed his assassin
Although the Duke of Bolton
Offered three hundred pounds' reward.

The crowd spat on Henry Luttrell's coffin.
Eighty years after his murder
Masked men, inspired by Wolfe Tone,
Burst open his tomb's locks,
Lit a stub of wax
And smashed the skull with a pickaxe.

Patrick Sarsfield's Portrait

Sarsfield, great-uncle in the portrait's grime,
Your emigration built your fame at home.
Landlord who never racked, you gave your rent
To travel with your mounted regiment.

Hotly you duelled for our name abroad
In Restoration wig, with German sword,
Wanting a vicious murder thrust to prove
Your Celtic passion and our Lady's love.

Gallant at Sedgemoor, cutting down for James
The scythe-armed yokels Monmouth led like lambs,
You thought it needed God's anointed king
To breathe our Irish winter into spring.

Your ashwood lance covered the Boyne retreat:
When the divine perfidious monarch's rout
From kindred enemy and alien friend
Darkened the land, you kindled Ireland.

At Limerick besieged, you led the dance:
'If this had failed, I would have gone to France.'
When youths lit brandy in a pewter dish
You were their hazel nut and speckled fish.

A French duke scoffed: 'They need no cannonballs
But roasted apples to assault these walls.'
Sarsfield, through plague and shelling you held out;
You saved the city, lost your own estate.

Shunning pitched battle was your strategy:
You chose rapparee mountain routes to try
The enemy's morale, and blew his train
Of cannon skywards in the soft night rain.

Your king, who gave St Ruth supreme command,
Mistrusted you, native of Ireland.
'Await further orders,' you were told
At Aughrim, when your plan was overruled.

You stood, while brother officers betrayed
By going, and six thousand Irish died.
Then you assumed command, but veered about:
Chose exile in your courteous conqueror's boat.

'Change kings with us, and we will fight again,'
You said, but sailed off with ten thousand men;
While women clutched the hawsers in your wake,
Drowning – it was too late when you looked back.

Only to come home stronger had you sailed:
Successes held you, and the French prevailed.
Coolly you triumphed where you wanted least,
On Flemish cornfield or at Versailles feast.

We loved you, horseman of the white cockade,
Above all, for your last words, 'Would to God
This wound had been for Ireland.' Cavalier,
You feathered with the wild geese our despair.

Battle Hill Revisited

Strangers visit the townland:
Called after wild geese, they fly through Shannon.

They know by instinct the sheepwalk
As it was before the great hunger and the exodus:

Also this cool creek of traitors.
They have come here to seek out ancestors.

They have read that the wind
Carried their forebears' gunsmoke, to make blind

The enemy, but nevertheless the Lord
Permitted the wicked to purify the good.

They know little about God
But something of the evil exploded by the word.

They are at the navel of an island
Driving slowly into well-drained battleground,

To follow the glacial esker
By a new signpost to the credal slaughter,

Blood on a stone altar.
Seed, there should be seed, buried in a cairn.

If they listen, they may hear
Rival prayers of their warring ancestors.

Soon they locate the dun
Where St Ruth spun the thread of his fatal plan.

They try to imagine
Exactly what took place, what it could mean,

Whether by will or by chance:
Then turn in time to catch a plane for France.

THE GOD WHO EATS CORN

At the end of the nineteenth century, the people who lived in the king-dom of Lobengula in central Africa, defined in their own language the first white men they had ever seen, who had arrived with guns to take over their country, as 'gods who eat corn'. These gods, who could kill from far off, they noticed, were subject as humans to hunger, desire, disease and death.

I

In his loyal garden, like Horace's farm,
He asks his visitors to plant a tree.
The black shadow of the African msasa
Squats among the lawn's colonial company.

In honour among watersprays that spin
Rainbows to keep alive old English roses
Hand-weeded by a docile piccanin
The Queen Mother's cypress nods in a straw hood.

The trees are labelled. A chairman of mines
Gave this copper beech, that silver oak
Was trowelled by a Governor: great names
Written on tags, Llewellin and Tredgold.

Livingstone's heir presented this wild fig
From the burnt-out forest of Africa:
On its branches by moonlight a boomslang swings.
This Cape creeper has a cold blue flower.

As a son I choose the native candelabra:
Perched on an ant-hill, after years of drought,
From its cut spines a milky sap flows.
I give my father this tree as a tribute.

His own plane tree, brought as a seed from Cos,
From the shade where Hippocrates swore his oath,
Wilts in the voodoo climate, while gum trees
The trekkers imported have sapped the earth.

Under these trees, he believes that indaba
Could heal the blood feud. Bullfrogs crackle
In the lily pond. Tolerant water
Eases roots, but cannot cool the racist fever.

II

From his green study half-door he looks out
On the young plantation of his old age;
An ibis is perched on a cone hut,
Rain-birds croak in a citrus orchard.

Boys are sharpening pangas at the wood-pile:
Trailers approach, filling barns from the field
With limp tobacco to be dried by steam.
A Union Jack droops on the school flag-pole.

Hunkered on dust in kaffir quarters
With rickety babies, the sewing club meets,
My mother bringing gifts through trellis doors
Frail as a lily in her straw sun-hat.

Such tinkle of bangles, such ivory teeth
Clacking, they gossip of clothes and clinics.
A child rolls a pram-wheel over the earth,
A cat is stalking the cooped-up chickens.

He drives to the store to collect his *Times*
And letters from home, tulip trees in flower,
Road grit on his tongue, tobacco booms
A memory, hot wind raising a dust-choked roar.

He swims before breakfast in a patio pool
Recalling Atlantic waves, a gothic half-light
Splashed on to hymn-books in a pitch-pine hall
Where his father preached. He prays at night.

At a carol service in the grading shed
He reads the lesson, joining trade with truth.
My knees remember his coconut mats,
The mesh of our duty to improve the earth.

III

'To do some good for this poor Africa'
Was Livingstone's prayer, but not the Founder's dream.
Towards gold and diamonds, the Pioneer Column
Trekked at the bidding of a childless millionaire.

They came with ox-wagons, claiming a treaty,
To Lobengula's kraal, his great indaba tree,
With charming letters from Queen Victoria:
There the chameleon swallowed the black fly.

In dusty dorps they slept with slave-girls,
On farms they divided the royal herd.
In stifling mine-shafts the disarmed warriors
Were flogged to work, their grazing grounds wired.

So now at white homesteads, the coffee steams
On creepered verandas. Racial partners
Do not mix in wedlock sons and daughters.
The white man rides: the black man is his horse.

Brown bare feet slide softly over the tiles
Soothing the master, scrubbing his bath,
Folding his towels, timidly with smiles
Smoothing his pillow, and wincing at his wrath.

To each black, his ten acres for millet,
To each white, his three thousand of grass:
The gospel of peace preached from the pulpit,
From the hungry fields the gospel of force.

IV

In a paradise for white gods he grows old
Cutting rafters out of the felled wood,
Baking bricks from the clay of ant-hills,
Planting the first rose on the burnt sandveld.

Thirteen years ago his library was unpacked
In the path of mambas, where bushmen's fire
Sooted their drawings on the walls of caves
And the sand was printed by lion spoor.

Walking for many days from parched Reserves
Africans came to work for food and money
To pay their poll-tax, mothers carrying children,
Calling him 'Baas', hungry and ill-at-ease.

They built wattle and clay rondavels to sleep in.
Tractors invaded the elephant road.
A bore-hole was sunk. Cicadas at his fly-screen
Halted and shrilled. The kudu retreated.

He fed corn to his gang and cured fever.
Cigarettes sold in a London shop
Kept people stooped on his kopje alive.
Each year he felled more trees to plant a crop.

Between the auction floors and seed-bed sowing
First in a thatched hut he began a school.
The market rose and fell, drought followed flooding,
When the leaves ripened there were showers of hail.

Daily at dawn, they clang the plough disc gong
That winds a chain of men through vleis and veld.
No boss-boy drives them with a sjambok's thong.
At dusk they come to class rooms to be schooled.

Children are chanting hymns, their lean bodies
Tropically sensual behind puritan desks,
From mealie plot and swamp of tsetse flies
Lured by the power of the god's mechanics.

A red-hot poker flowers in the playground,
A viper sleeps on the sand. The dry slate
Under the sweating palm is rubbed and scrawled.
They wait like logs, ready for fire and wind.

V

Tall in his garden, shaded and brick-walled,
He upholds the manners of a lost empire.
Time has confused dead honour with dead guilt
But lets a sunbird sip at a gold creeper.

His scholar's head, disguised in a bush hat,
Spectacled eyes that watch the weaver's nest
Woven, have helped a high dam to be built
Where once the Zambezi was worshipped and wasted.

Sometimes he dreams of a rogue elephant
That smashed the discharged rifle in his hand:
Or reading, remembers the horns of buffalo,
The leopards he shipped to the Dublin zoo.

While he reads Homer's *Iliad* in Greek
Rhodesian forces arm for a civil war.
Pyres are kindling under *Pax Britannica*
As black politicians school themselves in jail.

At dusk on his stoep he greets ambassadors
From Kenya and Ceylon. The silver trays
Are lit by candles cupped in flower borders.
Husks hang on his dry indaba trees.

Last thing at night he checks the rain-gauge
Remembering his father on a rectory lawn.
Thunder is pent in the drums of the compound.
He feels too old to love the rising moon.

1963

PART THREE

High Island

and poems of the years
1967-1973

Little Hunger

I drove to Little Hunger promontory
    Looking for pink stone
In roofless houses huddled by the sea
    To buy to build my own.

Hovels to live in, ruins to admire
    From a car cruising by,
The weathered face caught in a sunset fire,
    Hollowed with exility;

Whose gradual fall my purchase would complete,
    Clearing them off the land,
The seven cabins needed to create
    The granite house I planned.

Once mine, I'd work on their dismemberment,
    Threshold, lintel, wall;
And pick a hearthstone from a rubble fragment
    To make it integral.

Double Negative

(for Tony White)

You were standing on the quay
Wondering who was the stranger on the mailboat
While I was on the mailboat
Wondering who was the stranger on the quay

Pat Cloherty's Version of *The Maisie*

I've no tooth to sing you the song
    Tierney made at the time
        but I'll tell the truth

It happened on St John's Day
    sixty-eight years ago
        last June the twenty-fourth

The Maisie sailed from Westport Quay
    homeward on a Sunday
        missing Mass to catch the tide

John Kerrigan sat at her helm
    Michael Barrett stood at her mast
        and Kerrigan's wife lay down below

The men were two stepbrothers
    drownings in the family
        and all through the family

Barrett kept a shop in the island
    Kerrigan plied the hooker
        now deeply laden with flour

She passed Clare and she came to Cahir
    two reefs tied in the mainsail
        she bore a foresail but no jib

South-east wind with strong ebbtide
    still she rode   this way   that way
        hugging it   hugging it   O my dear

And it blew and blew hard and blew hard
  but Kerrigan kept her to it
    as long as he was there he kept her to it

Rain fell in a cloudburst
  hailstones hit her deck
    there was no return for him once he'd put out

At Inishturk when the people saw
  The Maisie smothered up in darkness
    they lit candles in the church

What more could Kerrigan do?
  he put her jaw into the hurricane
    and the sea claimed him

Barrett was not a sailor
  to take a man from the water
    yet the sea claimed him too

At noon the storm ceased
  and we heard *The Maisie*'d foundered
    high upon a Mayo strand

The woman came up from the forecastle
  she came up alone on deck
    and a great heave cast her out on shore

And another heave came while she drowned
  and put her on her knees
    like a person'd be in prayer

That's the way the people found her
  and the sea never came in
    near that mark no more

John Kerrigan was found
   far down at Achill Sound
      he's buried there

Michael Barrett was taken
   off Murrisk Pier
      he's buried there

Kerrigan's wife was brought from Cross
   home to Inishbofin
      and she's buried there

Walking on Sunday

Walking on Sunday into Omey Island
   When the tide had fallen slack
I crossed a spit of wet ribbed sand
   With a cold breeze at my back.

Two sheepdogs nosed me at a stile,
   Boys chevied on the green,
A woman came out of a house to smile
   and tell me she had seen

Men digging down at St Fechin's church,
   Buried in sand for centuries
Up to its pink stone gable top, a perch
   For choughs and sea-pies.

I found a dimple scalloped from a dune,
   A landing-slip for coracles,
Two graveyards – one for women, one for men –
   Odorous of miracles:

And twelve parishioners probing a soft floor
   To find what solid shape there was
Under shell-drift; seeking window, door;
   And measuring the house.

Blood was returning dimly to the face
   Of the chancel they'd uncovered,
Granite skin that rain would kiss
   Until the body flowered.

I heard the spades clang with a shock
   Inaugurating spring:
Fechin used plug and feather to split rock
   And poised the stone to sing.

He tuned cacophony to make
    Harmony in this choir:
The ocean gorged on it, he died of plague,
    And hawks nested there.

Omey Island

Was there a house or church for which these flesh-pink
Boulders were quarried but never used,
As if the builders had expired
Leaving random, irregular forms
Of a thousand years ago
To be dressed by vanished masons?

Or did no force but the sea
Split from solid rock these makings of ashlars,
And fling them above high watermark
To lie in confusion crying out
For hands to give them the grace of stonework
Lost in beehive cells buried under the sand?

With its loud mouth and sharp tongue the ocean
Explodes at the quarry-face of the shore
Without a notion of hearths, lintels and tombstones,
Gathering more and more power
To rampage over the island, or disgorge
Enough raw granite to face a whole new town.

Jurors

– Why did he kill her? Jealousy, anger, drink?
There's always more to it than what you hear.

– It had to happen, it was coming to her,
Unfortunate girl, since the day she was born.
He used to work as a turf cutter:
The man she left him for drove a van in town.

– Why are they taking so long to arrest
If they saw him follow her out of the hall
And found her shoe on the road, her body pressed
Head first into a stream behind a wall?

– They've sent away his boots to be analysed
And a few ribs they found of her chestnut hair.

Corncrake

Petty boss of a ditch
Why so much energy and such a boring song?
Surely your mate must be tired of hearing
How little you have to say
And how often you repeat yourself
Through the small hours of the night
While she is silently sitting on her nest
And producing your offspring
O yes, you're a hero to distract the attention
Of everyone away from her significant
Silent creation
By compelling us to listen to your cant
Though you really can't help it
You'd prefer to sing like the lark
But the only flying you can manage
Is involuntary migration
Trailing your fleshy feet behind you
Just clearing meadow and cornland
Dipping with relief into the nearest drain
Instead of upwards into the sun
And never where you're likely to be seen

Song for a Corncrake

Why weave rhetoric on your voice's loom,
Shuttling at the bottom of my garden
In meadowsweet and broom?
Crepuscular, archaic politician,
It's time to duck down,
Little bridegroom.

Why draft an epic on a myth of doom
In staunchly nailed iambics
Launched nightly near my room?
Since all you need to say is *crex*
Give us lyrics,
Little bridegroom.

Who go on chiselling mottoes for a tomb,
Counting on a scythe to spare
Your small defenceless home?
Quicken your tune, O improvise, before
The combine and the digger come,
Little bridegroom.

Epitaph for Shura

March 1969

> '*Who can but pity the merciful intention of those hands*
> *that do destroy themselves?*'

SIR THOMAS BROWNE

Before you'd given death a name
Like Bear or Crocodile, death came

To take your mother out one night.
But when she'd said her last good night

You cried, 'I don't want you to go,'
So in her arms she took you too.

Gallows Riddle

Hangman   In I went, out again,
Death I saw, life within,
Three confined there, one let free:
Riddle me that or hung you'll be.

Tinker   Five maggoty sheep I stole
Tangled me on the gallows tree,
Now my tongue must riddle me free:
A nest of birds in an old man's skull.

The Reading Lesson

Fourteen years old, learning the alphabet,
He finds letters harder to catch than hares
Without a greyhound. Can't I give him a dog
To track them down, or put them in a cage?
He's caught in a trap, until I let him go,
Pinioned by 'Don't you want to learn to read?'
'I'll be the same man whatever I do.'

He looks at a page as a mule balks at a gap
From which a goat may hobble out and bleat.
His eyes jink from a sentence like flushed snipe
Escaping shot. A sharp word, and he'll mooch
Back to his piebald mare and bantam cock.
Our purpose is as tricky to retrieve
As mercury from a smashed thermometer.

'I'll not read any more.' Should I give up?
His hands, longfingered as a Celtic scribe's,
Will grow callous, gathering sticks or scrap;
Exploring pockets of the horny drunk
Loiterers at the fairs, giving them lice.
A neighbour chuckles. 'You can never tame
The wild duck: when his wings grow, he'll fly off.'

If books resembled roads, he'd quickly read:
But they're small farms to him, fenced by the page,
Ploughed into lines, with letters drilled like oats:
A field of tasks he'll always be outside.
If words were banknotes, he would filch a wad;
If they were pheasants, they'd be in his pot
For breakfast, or if wrens he'd make them king.

Travelling Man

What can have held him on the road so long?
A fair, a camp in a quarry, horses,
Pubs, or a girl bathing under a bridge?
He may have met with a crowd
From Tourmakeady or Kiltimagh.
A guard may have given him a summons.
Better not ask, if he turns up,
Just offer shelter and food.
Your door will never be his destination:
Sometime if he's passing he may knock.

Walled Up

He danders down the forge lane
From the coastguard station to the shop
With a string bag for a message
They've told him to bring up,
And when he meets my garden wall
He asks, politely taking off his cap,
'How are the prisoners in Mountjoy Jail?'

The Glass Dump Road

A candle was burning in the caravan
Parked where three roads forked beside a mound
Of broken bottles near a market town.
A woman was tottering home
With a bundle of children's clothes and a loaf of bread
After closing time.
A campfire in the ditch was dying out.

She peeped into the tent and heard her children breathe.
A snipe drummed on the moor.
The wagon door was bolted. Why had he shut her out?
A bantam cock on the axle-tree
Opened his eyes and crowed.
She peered through a smirched pane of glass,
Fell on the ground and screamed.

A candle was burning beside the bed
Spilling wax on the table, guttering in the draught.
A man was kneeling naked
Over a naked child
Offering her his penis to play with like a toy.
Hearing a noise outside
He quickly stubbed the candle flame with his thumb.

A whippet chained to the axle growled.
A child woke in the wattle tent, and cried, 'Mammy!'
The caravan leaned silently as a tombstone
Over the woman lying prone on the mud
Weeping. What should she do?
The breeze tugged at a skirt hung on a thorn to dry.
She staggered down the road to fetch the Guards.

Childhood in Ceylon, *c*. 1933

1 *Firebug*

He's tired of winding up the gramophone
Halfway through 'Three Little Maids',
And waiting for a rickshaw to return from the bazaar.
The monsoon teems on the compound.
A coolie, splitting coconuts on an iron spike,
Stoops to wring the rain out of his loin-cloth.
The boy picks up a box of matches.

His little sister comes from the nursery holding a doll.
'Give me that!' 'What for?'
'I want to set it on fire.' 'You wouldn't dare.'
'I will if you help me.'
She puts the doll on the floor. He strikes a match
And holds it gingerly under the pink legs.
The girl screeches like a cockatoo.

The fire bursts into song,
Eats the doll, sticks out its tongue, stands up
Gyrating like a crimson top: then dies.
Burnt celluloid leaves a guilty smell.
The girl cries over the ashes, 'Give me back my doll!'
'An angel took it to heaven, didn't you see?'
The devil needs thrashing with a shoe.

2 *The Writing Lesson*

His finger smells of rubbings out and sharpened lead.
She's teaching him to write.
The table stands in little bowls of fluid
To keep down cockroach and termite.
Above them sags a ceiling cloth
Stained by civet cats prowling in the roof.
A punkah fans them ,while he copies *God Is Love*.

What are words made of? Squiggles, lines, dots.
Sweat spoils the page.
If he writes well, she'll give him a bicycle
To ride round the compound while his brother walks.
For silly mistakes, she'll rap his knuckles.
John's dusting the Crossley's khaki hood.
Let's go to the breakwater! Let's go to the Officer's Beach!

'Run out and play.' Appu's cooking curry for lunch.
He stands under a flowering temple tree
Looking up at a coppersmith perched on a branch:
Crimson feathers, pointed beard.
All day long it hammers at a single word.
Is it bored? Is it learning?
Why can't it make a sentence, or break into song?

3 *Coppersmith*

A temple tree grew in our garden in Ceylon.
We knew it by no other name.
The flower, if you turned it upside down,
Looked like a dagoba with an onion dome.
A holy perfume
Stronger than the evil tang of betelnut
Enticed me into its shade on the stuffiest afternoon,

Where I stood and listened to the tiny hammerstroke
Of the crimson coppersmith perched above my head,
His *took took took*
And his *tonk tonk tonk*
Were spoken in a language I never understood:
And there I began to repeat
Out loud to myself an English word such as beat beat beat,

Till hammering too hard I lost the meaning in the sound
Which faded and left nothing behind,
A blank mind,
The compound spinning round,
My brain melting, as if I'd stood in the sun
Too long without a topee and was going blind,
Till I and the bird, the word and the tree, were one.

4 *The Fall*

Thunder in the patanas. He's falling off a cliff.
Every branch he catches breaks.
Down he hurtles, counting... one... two... then wakes
In the nick of time. His heart pounds with relief.
It's Nanny's afternoon off.
He untucks his mosquito net
And shakes the fear of scorpions from his shoes.

Hours to go, nothing to do but wait.
A tom-tom roars at the Temple of the Tooth.
He peeps at the bathroom coolie rinsing a pot,
Picks up his cat
And saunters out on the upstairs nursery verandah.
'Would Marmalade die if he fell from this height?'
A bullock-bandy creaks past the compound gate.

'Why don't you try it?' his brother says.
'Cats have four feet to land on: they're not like us.'
He hugs the warm purring bag
Of muscle, fur and bone.
'Suppose it kills him?' 'I dare you to do it.'
The boy holds his pet over the green balustrade
And lets go.

The legs fly out like an X. Marmalade pancakes
And lies dead still on the lawn.
A wanderoo gibbers in the crown of a royal palm.
'Look! he's alive: I saw him twitch.'
They rush downstairs
In time to see the cat
Vanish near a snake-hole under a jasmine hedge.

That night he walks to the chair with long wooden arms;
Whisky glass, tobacco pouch, crossword puzzle, pen;
To own up like a gentleman.
Scent of cartridges ejected from a shotgun,
Glint of pince-nez, mosaic frown.
The hand with a gold signet ring bends him down,
A lion rampant on a little hairy finger.

Out in the jungle beyond the fire-fly net
Poochies are biting Marmalade, sucking his blood.
Tuck up tight.
'I'm not going to kiss you tonight, naughty boy.'
Do all experiments go phut?
Early in the morning kitchen coolies shout.
Marmalade walks in purring…four unbroken feet.

5 *Kandy Perahera*

You take off your new blancoed shoes at the temple door.
She wraps them in tissue paper,
Humming her favourite bar of 'Pomp and Circumstance'.
Lightly your feet slip, feeling the cool marble floor.
'Stop showing off! Remember where you are!'
Flambeaux, tom-yoms, flageolets, incense.
Devil-dancers, with a clash of cymbals, begin to dance.

They hobble and sway above you on bamboo stilts:
Crocodile, panther, jackal, monkey, toad:
Tongues hanging out, paddystraw hair, boils and welts
On bums with tails, torsos gummy as rubber trees,
Jungle-fowl feathers glued on thighs.
Each bears the spots or sores of an incurable disease.
Copper bells clang on elbows, ankles and knees.

They block the corridor you've got to pass. Their sweat
Steams like monsoon rain on a path of dust.
Coconut cressets, carried by almost naked men,
Burn with a sickening fume.
'Nan, I'm thirsty. Can't we go home?'
Your mouth is as dry as pith on a mango stone.
You turn and bury your head in her old green gown.

She smarms your hair, tightens the knot in your silk tie:
Takes you out on a high cool balcony
Freed from the ant-hill crowd.
Huge howdahed elephants lumber out of a wood,
Trapped under jewelled caparisons. Gongs and floodlight.
'When I grow up, will you let me marry you?'
'By the time you're old enough, I'll be buried in Timbuktu.'

A monk hangs a garland of temple flowers round your neck.
Tea planters chatter and smoke.
'How did the Tooth fit in Buddha's mouth?'
'It must be a tiger's. Nobody knows the truth.'
Can't you see which elephant carries the holy relic?
Pain jabs your heart. Poison! You almost cry.
Doesn't she realise: Won't she believe? You're going to die.

A pigeon's blood ruby sparkles in Lady Weerasirie's nose.
Hum of malarial mosquitoes.
Worse and worse the pain. 'Can we go home soon?'
At the temple door you put on your shoes.
A monk in a saffron robe is watching you. 'Goodbye.'
Mind you don't step on a scorpion.
Full moon, treefrogs, fireflies: a brutal jungle cry.

Your throat's burning. Will there be time to reach home
And call Dr Chisel? Look, here's a traveller's palm.
She shows you the place to sink
The point of the ivory penknife you won in a race:
A dark olive leaf-sheath curving out of a dry old stem.
If you die, can you be reborn? Try!
Even if the water of the tree is poison, drink!

High Island

A shoulder of rock
Sticks high up out of the sea,
A fisherman's mark
For lobster and blue-shark.

Fissile and stark
The crust is flaking off,
Seal rock, gull rock,
Cove and cliff.

Dark mounds of mica schist,
A lake, mill and chapel,
Roofless, one gable smashed,
Lie ringed with rubble.

An older calm,
The kiss of rock and grass,
Pink thrift and white sea-campion,
Flowers in the dead place.

Day keeps lit a flare
Round the north pole all night.
Like brushing long wavy hair
Petrels quiver in flight.

Quietly as the rustle
Of an arm entering a sleeve,
They slip down to nest
Under altar stone or grave.

Round the wrecked laura
Needles flicker
Tacking air, quicker and quicker
To rock, sea and star.

Brian Boru's Well

This well is holy but looks foul.
I clean it seven times a year,
Shovelling quicklime in the shade.
It fills mysteriously dark red.
Once I found a drowned wheatear
And once an old ram's skull.

How does it rise on top of a hill
And why is it never clear?
By miracle, tradition said:
Instead of springing, the rock shed
A slow continual tainted tear
Since Brian Boru's fall.

It was named by St Gormgall,
Hermit, lion, poet, seer
And king's confessor. When it bled
He knew his penitent was dead.
He saw millennial daybreak tear
Unwinding from its spool.

Even in drought it will not fail
But bless or curse. Don't interfere!
A bigot sledged the crystal bed:
Next day he shot his son in the head
Wild fowling. I cut outlets there
To keep it drinkable.

High Island pivots on this pool.
If a fly walks on the water
All's well with your friend abroad.
It quenched St. Brendan's thirst on board
When he touched here to pray before
Setting out for Hy Brasil.

Around the random horseshoe wall
I helped a mason to repair,
Pennies, fish-hooks, pins corrode.
A thousand years this carved stone stood
Beside the well, giving it power
To comfort or to heal.

Ball's Cove

Leaving her family at the lake
To dawdle over their antiquarian picnic,
She took Mr Ball to the top of a cliff
On the ocean side, and said as a joke:
'The man I marry must prove he's brave.
Go out and stand on that beak of rock
And turn three times on your heel.
You'll have my money, if all goes well.'

An hour later, she came back
Without Mr Ball. She looked terrified.
'I tried to talk him out of suicide.
He asked three times for my hand.
I told him I hadn't made up my mind,
And then he threatened
To throw himself over a ghastly cliff.
Before I could stop him, he'd gone.'

The coroner helped. 'A sad accident.'
The boatmen kept silent,
Well paid
By those grand people who came from abroad.
But a lobster fisherman said:
'She pushed him off,
I can prove it. I was near the cove
Hauling pots, and I heard her laugh.'

Granite Globe

Straining my back
Seven times I've lifted you
Up to my thighs

There are men
Who've put you sitting
High on their shoulders

It looks as if you'd been
Lopped
Off the top of a column

Then used as a quern
Kicked around
Buried

An archaeologist
Taped you
And wrote you down

He said
You're an oblate spheroid
Does it matter?

Whoever carved you
Gave you all
The time in the world

Stormpetrel

Gipsy of the sea
In winter wambling over scurvy whaleroads,
Jooking in the wake of ships,
A sailor hooks you
And carves his girl's name on your beak.

Guest of the storm
Who sweeps you off to party after party,
You flit in a sooty grey coat
Smelling of must
Barefoot across a sea of broken glass.

Waif of the afterglow
On summer nights to meet your mate you jink
Over sea-cliff and graveyard,
Creeping underground
To hatch an egg in a hermit's skull.

Pulse of the rock
You throb till daybreak on your cryptic nest
A song older than fossils,
Ephemeral as thrift.
It ends with a gasp.

Sunup

The sun kisses my eyes open:
Another day of wanting you.
I'd like to kiss your eyes again,
No comfort now in being alone.

Is she delighting you in bed
In her caravan on a cutaway road?
Does the sun give you the same kiss
To wake you, with her at your side?

I kiss you both, like the sun,
I kiss your hands and your feet,
Your ears and your eyes,
Both your bodies, I bless them both.

Do you feel this when you make love?
Do you love her as I loved you?
Will you let her steal all you have
And suffer her to leave?

Meet me today! We'll find a wood
Of blackthorn in white bud:
And let me give you one more kiss
Full of sun, free of bitterness.

Nocturne

The blade of a knife
Is tapped gently on an oak table
Waves are sobbing in coves

Light bleeds on the sky's rim
From dusk till dawn
Petrels fly in from the ocean

Wings beating on stone
Quick vibration of notes   throats   tongues
Under silverweed   calling   and calling

Louder cries cut the air
They rise from a pit
Complaints are retched up   and lost

A solo tune
Is dying with passion
From someone out there to come quickly

Come back!   come back!
I'm here   here   here
This burrow   this   wall this hole

Ach!   who kept you?   where've you been?
There   there   there
It's all over   over   over

Seals at High Island

The calamity of seals begins with jaws.
Born in caverns that reverberate
With endless malice of the sea's tongue
Clacking on shingle, they learn to bark back
In fear and sadness and celebration.
The ocean's mouth opens forty feet wide
And closes on a morsel of their rock.

Swayed by the thrust and backfall of the tide,
A dappled grey bull and a brindled cow
Copulate in the green water of a cove.
I watch from a cliff-top, trying not to move.
Sometimes they sink and merge into black shoals;
Then rise for air, his muzzle on her neck,
Their winged feet intertwined as a fishtail.

She opens her fierce mouth like a scarlet flower
Full of white seeds; she holds it open long
At the sunburst in the music of their loving;
And cries a little. But I must remember
How far their feelings are from mine marooned.
If there are tears at this holy ceremony
Theirs are caused by brine and mine by breeze.

When the great bull withdraws his rod, it glows
Like a carnelian candle set in jade.
The cow ripples ashore to feed her calf;
While an old rival, eyeing the deed with hate,
Swims to attack the tired triumphant god.
They rear their heads above the boiling surf,
Their terrible jaws open, jetting blood.

At nightfall they haul out, and mourn the drowned,
Playing to the sea sadly their last quartet,
An improvised requiem that ravishes
Reason, while ripping scale up like a net:
Brings pity trembling down the rocky spine
Of headlands, till the bitter ocean's tongue
Swells in their cove, and smothers their sweet song.

PART FOUR

Care

and poems of the years
1974-1984

Moonshine

To think
I must be alone:
To love
We must be together.

I think I love you
When I'm alone
More than I think of you
When we're together.

I cannot think
Without loving
Or love
Without thinking.

Alone I love
To think of us together:
Together I think
I'd love to be alone.

Care

Kidded in April above Glencolumbkille
On a treeless hill backing north, she throve
Sucking milk off heather and rock, until

I came with children to buy her. We drove
South, passing Drumcliff. Restless in the car,
Bleating, she gulped at plastic teats we'd shove

Copiously in her mouth. Soon she'd devour
Whatever we'd give. Prettily she poked
Her gipsy head with hornbuds through barbed wire

To nip off pea-tops, her fawn pelt streaked
With Black Forest shadow and Alpine snow.
I stalled her wildness in a pen that locked.

She grew tame and fat, fed on herbs I knew
Her body needed. We ransacked Kylemore
To bring her oak leaf, ivy and bark to chew.

I gutted goat books, learning how to cure
Fluke, pulpy kidney, black garget, louping ill:
All my attention bled to cope with her.

No commonage to roam unfenced, no hill
Where she could vanish under a dark cloud
To forage with a puckled flock: but the shrill

Grind of small children bucketing her food,
Yelling across a yard. Out in a forest
She would have known a bad leaf from a good.

Here, captive to our taste, she'd learnt to trust
The petting hand with crushed oats, or a new
Mash of concentrates, or sweet bits of waste.

So when a child mistook a sprig of yew
And mixed it with her fodder, she descried
No danger: we had tamed her instinct too.

Whiskey, white of egg, linseed oil, we tried
Forcing down antidotes. Nothing would do.
The children came to tell me when she died.

Trouvaille

This root of bog-oak the sea dug up she found
Poking about, in old age, and put to stand
Between a snarling griffin and a half-nude man
Moulded of lead on my chimneypiece.
It looks like a heron rising from a pond,
Feet dipped in brown trout water,
Head shooting arrowsharp into blue sky.

'What does it remind you of?' she wanted to know.
I thought of trees in her father's demesne
Levelled by chainsaws;
Bunches of primroses I used to pick
Before breakfast, hunting along a limestone lane,
To put at her bedside before she woke;
And all my childhood's broken promises.

No, no! It precedes alphabets,
Planted woods, or gods.
Twisted and honed as a mind that never forgets
It lay dead in bog acids, undecayable:
Secretively hardening in a womb of moss, until
The peat burnt off, a freak tide raised
The feathered stick she took to lure me home.

Mary Ure

Bare feet she dips across my boat's blue rail
In the ocean as we run under full white summer sail.
The cold spray kisses them. She's not immortal.

Sitting in her orchard she reads 'Lady Lazarus'
Aloud rehearsing, when her smallest child lays
Red peonies in her lap with tender apologies.

She walks by Lough Mask in a blue silk gown
So thin the cloudy wind is biting to the bone
But she talks as lightly as if the sun shone.

Shelter

Girl with a sheaf of rye-straw in your arms
How much you carry from a loaded trailer
Parked at the door in a stray sunny shaft
At the tail end of summer, deep into the barn
To store for thatch, if ever we get the weather
Or the time, before winter sets in, how much
You help me, child, in the hour after school,
Hour of your release, face wet with tears
That well up out of a cruelty done to you,
Bruise marks around your lips, a speechless harm,
How much you help me to make the dark inside
Glitter with sheaves bound firm to keep out storm.
Hear how they rustle as we lay them down:
Their broken heads are thrashed clean of grain.

Scythe

In a small meadow between outcrops of granite
   above a church that's buried in sand
     on Omey Island
An old farmer, who has lived here all his life
   without a machine, is teaching
     at my request
A tinker whose tribe has never owned land
   how to hold and handle
     a scythe.

They are cutting hay for the tinker's goats
   in the driest summer, Joeen says,
     since 1921
When tinsmiths were welcome on remote farms
   before plastic made them pariahs
     people hoped
The county council would settle decently in houses
   but not in our parish, heaven help us
     not next door!

As I watch them, a glint of sun catches
   the edge of a scythe upturned
     for the whetstone.
Be careful of your fingers, Paddy Oilcake!
   You know how to sharpen a knife
     to cut tobacco
But not this primordial blade of the farmer
   you might quit travelling
     to become.

How easy it looks! How relaxed the expert's
   arms and shoulders oscillating
     on the pivot of hips,

Heel of the scythe not scraping the ground
    as it sweeps back and forth
        sprung like a timepiece
Advancing swathe by swathe over warrior grasses,
   cocksfoot and crested dogstail,
      their plumes laid low.

Niches

Lovers I've lost are sleeping in the house I've left
To live alone in a cave with two glass entrances,
A skylight in the roof over a chair that broods
At the bottom of a well of sunshine on clear days,
Or a pit of night kept warm by a peat fire
When hailstones jitter, as now with a northerly gale
Squalling through cracks in my costly new shell:
While two calm urns of white Cycladic clay
Stand silently still in niches I drew last summer
In the random warm granite of my chimney breast.
A woman threw them lovingly, glazed them in tears,
Fired them one sleepless night, and put them here to stay
For ever. Now she's dismantled her wheel and gone.
Niched above my head I'll keep her bone-ash jars.

Swallows

She wades through wet rushes,
Long autumn grass,
Over rusty barbed wire
And stone walls that collapse,

With a black rubber torch
Flickering on and off,
After midnight, to reach
A shed with a tin roof.

She lifts away door boards –
O sweet herbal hay!
Her beam dazzles birds
She can't identify.

Timorous wings in wormy rafters
Flap to get out.
Then she spots in a light shaft
A red boot unlaced.

The flock's tremor increases
In her torch's coop.
Where is he? She sees
A white arm sticking up.

Stone Mania

How much it hurts me to tidy up when all my papers are
    heaped on the desk in a threemonth mess,
To regain control of this drift of days I've lost in
    my passion for building in granite,
And face the bills I must pay by leaving the house
    that has cost me too much to enlarge,
Where I passed the time too quickly preparing a place for
    the future to work within soundproof walls,
So never had a moment in the present for writing about
    the moments that were passing away:
How much it hurts to see the destruction that all good
    building, even the best, must cause,
Not only the hedges that had to be first cut down
    before the foundations were dug,
But deeper cuts through veins in the mind that carried
    the blood of memory through the brain:
How much it hurts me to have neglected all this summer
    the friends whom I might have seen,
But for my mad obsession of building more rooms
    to entertain them in time to come:
Because these times are apt to elude us, we die, or our
    friends drop dead before we can say
I'd love you to see and enjoy the house whose construction
    has kept us entirely apart.

Husbandry

Sheep like to graze on headlands
High up looking down on a raging sea.
It makes me dizzy to watch
An old ewe
Leaning over the edge to reach with her black mouth
A tuft of grass fine as hair.
I'd have to crawl there clutching frail stems.

How many of the flock fall
Dashed on to rocks or drowned in surf
To satisfy a peculiar hunger.
No soft herb
Pleases them as much as the spikes of gorse.
If I were their shepherd
I'd put them to fatten in a small safe paddock.

A Nest in a Wall

Smoky as peat your lank hair on my pillow
Burns like a tinker's fire in a mossy ditch.
Before I suffocate, let me slowly suck
From your mouth a tincture of mountain ash,
A red infusion of summer going to seed.
Ivy-clumps loosen the stonework of my heart.
Come like a wood-pigeon gliding there to roost!

I float a moment on a gust sighing for ever
Gently over your face where two swans swim.
Let me kiss your eyes in the slate-blue calm
Before their Connemara clouds return.
A spancelled goat bleats in our pleasure ground.
A whippet snarls on its chain. The fire dies out.
Litter of rags and bottles in the normal rain.

Your country and mine, love, can it still exist?
The unsignposted hawthorn lane of your body
Leads to my lichenous walls and gutted house.
Earth has almost lost your kind of beauty.
Although we have no home in the time that's come,
Coming together we live in our own time.
Make your nest of moss like a wren in my skull.

Tony White

1930-1976

Growing, he saw his friends increase
   Their incomes, houses, families,
   And saw this growth as a disease
Nothing but unpossessive love could cure.
Possessing nothing, he was not possessed
   By things or people, as we are.
      His granite chimney breast
Warmed friend or stranger at its open fire.
      There was no air
   Too foul for him to breathe, no pit
     Too dark to enter, yet
His very breathing made the foul air pure,
His presence made the darkest day feel clear.

He lived at the hub and not the rim
   Of time. Within himself he moved
Deeper towards dangerous ideas he loved
     To moot with bodily risk:
   Flying too close to the sun's disk,
   Sailing at night over a coral reef,
     Ghosting a thief's life.
      Since he's gone
No words of mine can rivet him to one
Role of some fortynine he used to play
    For pleasure more than pay.
Because his kind of love taught me to live
     His dying I forgive.

Tony White at Inishbofin

1959

With lobster-pot for a chair
And a fish-box for a table
He'd sacrificed a plausible career
On the London stage to live near
The sea in a bare room
Far from home
To become on the lips of islanders a fable.

In an old pair of black jeans
Threadbare though tautly darned
By himself needling with a woman's patience
Buckled in a looted Hun's
Eagle and swastika belt
Disguised he felt
Reborn as a fisherman whose craft he learned.

From an off-white Aran sweater
Knitted by his neighbour's wife
His dark face opened like a long loveletter
That makes a forlorn reader
Revive with a gust of hope
While he moused rope
For crayfish traps with a horn gutting knife.

Through panes of cobwebbed glass
Across a lime-washed stone sill
He hauled in shoals of riffled sun to please
Only a few friends like us
Because it was his style
To play as well
Carrying a creel on his back, or Coriolanus.

Bookcase for *The Oxford English Dictionary*

All the words I need
Stored like seed in a pyramid
To bring back from the dead your living shade
Lie coffined in this thing of wood you made
Of solid pine mortised and glued
Not long before you died.

Words you'll never read
Are good for nothing but to spread
Your greater love of craft in word and deed,
A gift to make your friends' desires succeed
While inwardly with pain you bled
To keep your own pride hid.

Circles

These are rocks he loved when he was alive
And how alive he was, like the sun this afternoon
Making mica gleam on the cold face of granite
And giving walls a long shadow across the grass
In the dead of winter, when he'd come from abroad
Like the sun emerging now from behind that cloud
To flood this dark lake water with golden light,
So that I still believe in him as in the sun,
And expect him to reappear as winter passes,
The telephone ringing some stormy night, his voice
Calmly announcing the day he's planning to cross
Back into our lives with so much news to tell
Of where he has been since he died, though I know
It's only a dream, so vivid it makes me cry
'Tony, it's you! What the hell made you play
This trick on us? Thank God you're alive and well!'
Which cannot be, though the sun breaks through
All the clouds on the lake where I cast his ashes
And a heron rose from these rocks like a ghost
In three wide circles ascending who knows where.

The Afterlife

Two swans take off from the wind-ruffled
Water of a pond below my hexagon
And a heron glides down to poise on a rock
In a clump of reeds and waterlilies.

With his long grey neck stretched out he sees
All the eyes in the country
That are looking at him, including
Mine through the lenses of binoculars.

It scares and compels him to change his perch
To a half-rotted stake that no longer
Supports a barbed wire fence
Between neighbours at loggerheads.

In a dark liquid circle he turns
The power of his vision on the silt
Of decades muddying the bottom
Where fish he dreams about lie embedded.

Now I can only see the top of his head
Far off pointing down. Could this be the bird
That soared from a rock in lake water
As our friend's ashes broke out of your pot?

Morning Call

Up from trawlers in the fish dock they walk to my house
On high-soled clogs, stepping like fillies back from a forge
Newly shod, to wake me at sunrise from a single bed
With laughter peeling skin from a dream ripening on mossy
Branches of my head – 'Let us in!' 'Let us in!' – and half naked
I stumble over books on the floor to open my door of glass
To a flood that crosses the threshold, little blue waves

Nudging each other, dodging rocks they've got to leap over,
Freshening my brackish pools, to tell me of 'O Such a night
Below in the boats!' 'We can't go home! What *will* they say?'
Can I think of a lie to protect them from God only knows
What trouble this will cause, what rows? 'We'll run away
And never come back!' – till they flop into black armchairs,
Two beautiful teenage girls from a tribe of tinkers,

Lovely as seals wet from fishing, hauled out on a rock
To dry their dark brown fur glinting with scales of salmon
When the spring tide ebbs. This is their everlasting day
Of being young. They bring to my room the sea's iodine odour
On a breeze of voices ruffling my calm as they comb their long
Hair tangled as weed in a rock pool beginning to settle clear.
Give me the sea-breath from your mouths to breathe a while!

Sea Holly

Thrives upon sand where no other plant can live
Close to high water mark on haggard shores,
And crops up briefly in summer wearing stiff
Armour embossed with mauve and sapphire flowers.
All the rest of the year it spends underground
In stupefying torpor. How can it raise
Enough energy to rise above the sand
Piled over it by waves, and open its eyes?
Like yours, the colour of hurt, they want to hide
Until in a blaze of blue spikes they explode.

Quays

Waiting for the sun to rise in Syracuse, New York,
the snow to melt and a term of grief to pass,
I think of boys who sailed with me
from deserted quays at Rosroe and Cleggan,
Inishturk and Renvyle, Bofin and Shark,
long grown distant from tidal heaves
that broke over our bows
at the Leahy Rocks, Cuddoo and Carrigmahog,
having wives and children to look after
with cars and television,
no more hand-hauling anchor chains, as when
for sheer love and small money
we toiled with rods and hand-lines
far out kedging for pollock on shoals by day,
then cabined in the dark, our warps made fast
to bollards on a slippery fish-gut-tainted quay,
where the sea gave an odd suckling sigh
as it ebbed from the dock
and our hull, bruised against a wall of barnacles,
used to groan as we came to rest.

Arsonist

The summer visitors have gone.
Rain blathers at the glass.
He drifts alone
On the sound-waves of his vacant house.

So firm his tongued and grooved oak floors!
By his building he's possessed.
His dark teak doors
Creak as they close him in his past.

Each random stone made integral
Has bonded him with debt.
All he can feel
Is a dying to get rid of it.

With craft to burn, how could he use
Control to lose control,
To spark a blaze
Spontaneous and elemental?

Fire would transmute his home in hours
To a foetiferous void,
A mould that flowers
Gravid with fronds of gutter lead.

Elixir

Turning a stone house into seven figures
Transported him to money's clean cold alp
To hang-glide on a market's thermal rigours
Learning new ways to corner, hedge or scalp.

Turning a copper nail that tightly gripped
A green slate on his roof to daily bread
Made him afraid to eat when sterling dipped
And meat cost more than doorlocks or sheet lead.

Turning a life's work into stocks and shares
Converted him to shirk the tears and shocks
Of love, rid of laborious household cares
And freed him to buy sex on piers and docks.

Turning old granite walls to bars of gold
Amassed his fears of sudden falls in one
Commodity. When all his wealth was told
It filled a vault with bone-dry speculation.

Turning his home into a foreign room
Replete with art to beat inflation chilled
His heart to zero. In that ice-bound tomb
He housed immortal seed unsowed, untilled.

Amsterdam

Money was evil:
Therefore he locked up large sums of it in gold,
   In ships and warehouses,
   Polders and dikes,
To hold back the leviathan and the flood,
To stop it corrupting poor people
   Who might have bought luxuries,
   Drugs and whores,
Or wasted their lives enjoying themselves.

How his capital has grown!
Where he used to sit at night in his room
   With no curtains drawn
   To show next-door neighbours
His gloomy interior had nothing evil to hide,
A girl from the Far East with her breasts bare
   Sits stoned in red light
   And a strange greasy flood
Leaches into her parlour with money to burn.

Altar

Blocking the way to get behind the house
To climb crooked stone steps to see the view
A huge grey granite boulder lay. With you
To help, I'd shift the obstacle with ease.

Was it a Mass rock blessed in penal days
Better left undisturbed? Too near the wall
It made our bedroom weep. Too flat to roll
It caught a bulldozer between two trees.

A granite mason told us to use fire
And water. One calm Sunday we piled coal
To heaven. Then doused the hot slab from a pool.
Not a seam cracked. Instead, we'd fouled the air.

Chagrined, we tried digging a deep wide pit;
Eased down the bald obtruder; buried it.

Displaced Person

Those years ago, when I made love to you,
   With fears I was afraid you knew,
   To grow strong I'd pretend to be
A boy I'd loved, loving yourself as me.
I played his part so open-eyed that you
   Believed my artful ploy was true.
To show I'd nothing false to hide
And make you feel the truth of love I lied.

The love of truth made me confess, and died
   Exposing my hermetic guide,
   A youth found loitering in the mart
Of memory's torndown inner city heart.
I feel betrayed by dead words that decide
   If head or tail be certified.
   Dear girl, come back and take a new
Lover in me, let him make love to you.

Visiting Hour

(for Thomas Kinsella in 1980)

How can I comfort you? What can I say?
You seem so far away, though near me now,
Sedated in that iron bed
Behind a curtain I'm afraid to draw:
With languished head
Propped on a pillow, mute and weak.
Would it be better not to speak?

Do you remember the day
We drifted west of Cleggan Bay
In the slack of tide, a fish on every hook:
The crossed lines and the lost
Leads, and seagulls scrawling around the mast
That listed while waves yeasted over a rock:
The gutted pollock gasping on our deck?

At least your poetry will stay unblurred.
Stuck with needles in this ward,
No peasant shoulders to support your feet,
You lie and fret. Work incomplete.
Tubes in your throat. And this is you,
Who put flesh into words that can't renew
The life you lavished making them ring true.

PART FIVE

The Price of Stone
a sequence of 50 sonnets
1981-1984

for Dennis O'Driscoll

Between April 1981 and November 1983 at 'Knockbrack', an isolated house on Mullen's Hill in Killiney, I wrote the following sequence of fifty sonnets called 'The Price of Stone'. Each sonnet, except 'Natural Son', speaks as a different persona emanating from a building associated with my life.

The process involved continuous writing of notes evoking more and more memories. I wrote with a fountain pen on the centimetre-squared pages of a small French notebook, which seemed to provide a better-than-blank worksheet for metrical poetry. While examining my life, I tried to circumvent inhibition and embarrassment by addressing 'myself' as 'you'. Hence came the different voices of the 'sonnet-houses'.

And with each sonnet I tried to condense pages of ventriloquised autobiography into fourteen lines of rhyming or off-rhyming verse. I thought of the process as rain on a moor filling streams that converge at a rock to produce a waterfall, as at 'Lecknavarna'.

Folly

I rise from a circle standing on a square
And cock my dunce's cap at the firmament
Keeping my ignorance tapered to a clear
Sugarloaf point above the dark green ferment.

A lord's pride made me to relieve the poor
With heavy work lifting my spire, and the rich
With light step ascending my gazebo stair
To admire the land they owned and wish for more.

My form is epicene: male when the gold
Seed of the sun comes melting through my skin
Of old grey stucco: female when the mould
Of moonlight makes my witch-pap cone obscene.

My four doors bricked up against vandals, still
Tumescent, scrawled with muck, I crest the hill.

Lead Mine Chimney

Pointlessly standing up to make a pointed
Remark on a skyline everyone can see
Not puffing smoke out any more, disjointed
By age, I speak of cut stone symmetry.

Remember when you look at my cold grey stack
I took the heart from oak woods to smelt ore,
Made people richer, poorer. Now I lack
The guts to pour out sulphur and hot air.

When you've poked your head inside my bevelled flue,
Inhaled a sooty chill of hollowness,
You'll know I've lost the fury to renew
The furnace at my root, all that foul stress.

Clearly I'll go on uttering, while I may,
In granite style, with not a word to say.

Portico

A dark headland hangs in a beady noose
Of mercury vapour across a bay of mud.
All night, solitary shadows of men cruise
My concrete cloister, ghosts questing blood.

I perch on rocks by the cineritious sea
Fossilised in decay: no painted porch
For a stoic mind, no shore temple of Shiva,
But a new kind of succursal, deviate church.

My spumy grotto's hooded devotees,
Sucked in a black hole that the sea has scoured,
Perform on flutes groping, mute melodies
With a seedy touch of ithyphallic art.

My hymns are hog-snorts, squealing bottle-glass
Screwed underfoot, a wave's foghorn caress.

Nelson's Pillar

My duty done, I rose as a Doric column
Far from at home, planted to reach the sky;
A huge stake in the crossed heart of a glum
Garrison city overlooked by my blind eye.

One-armed on a cold square abacus to rule
The waves, I never controlled the verminous
Poor beggars round my plinth, schooled to rebel.
I was loved well as a tramway's terminus.

Who cares, now, what good masons carved my four
Sea victories in granite from Golden Hill?
When masked men cracked my head off, the blast wore
Red, white and blue in a flash of puerile skill.

Dismasted and dismissed, without much choice,
Having lost my touch, I'll raise my chiselled voice.

Wellington Testimonial

Needling my native sky over Phoenix Park
I obelise the victory of wit
That let my polished Anglo-Irish mark
Be made by Smirke, as a colossal spit.

Properly dressed for an obsolete parade,
Devoid of mystery, no winding stair
Threading my unvermiculated head,
I've kept my feet, but lost my nosey flair.

My life was work: my work was taking life
To be a monument. The dead have won
Capital headlines. Look at Ireland rife
With maxims: need you ask what good I've done?

My sole point in this evergreen oak aisle
Is to maintain a clean laconic style.

Georgian Tenement

The high court of dry rot, after a long
Unreportable session behind airtight doors,
Has mouthed a verdict. Rafters know what's wrong.
Death and cremation. Up with my soft floors.

I've got to be rebuilt. Some new, banal
Office block is decreed to fill my place.
The whores under the trees by the canal
Increase their turnover while I lose face.

Young lovers of old structures, you who squat
To keep my form intact, when the Guards arrive
With riot gear and water gun, we cannot
Under such tonnage of cracked slate survive.

Would that your free hands in my spongy wood
Could cure fungosity, make my flaws good.

Gym

Vice-regal walls dominate the back street
Where men, succumbing to my spurious name
For body culture, enter in retreat
From words that shame, to act a heartless mime.

Discreetly couched, taking no verbal risk,
Ingled in clutches masked by sauna steam,
Nude club members, immune from women, bask
In tableaux mixed with musak, cocaine, jism.

See how my fabric, full of cock and bull,
Grotesquely free, though ruled by symmetry,
Lays you in some small penetralian cell
To come to grief, past all immunity.

The powers that be, served covertly by AIDS,
Strip to the bone your skin-deep masquerades.

Knockbrack

When driven to explore a strange blind alley
First clambering footloose up a speckled hill
You gambled on rare views of infilled valley,
Blossom of Chinese tang on a thorny grill.

Coming to speculate, you stayed for good:
Your fortune in the gold market of whins.
Avuncular pines admonished you to brood
On dark tale ends with woodcut colophons.

A spirited father walked barefoot to Rome:
A son died sniffing glue. Nobody lasted.
Well finished as rifle bolts at the Somme
My door-locks made you feel safely invested.

Grey granite cropped up an archaic head
To check your feet, your line of living dead.

Ice Rink

Reflections of a spotlit mirror-ball,
Casting a light net over a pearl pond
In oval orbits, magnify my haul
Of small fry at a disco, coiled in sound.

On anticlockwise tracks, all shod with steel,
Initiates feel exalted; starlets glide
To cut more ice with convoluted skill
Practising tricks that lure them to backslide.

Their figure-carving feet have chased my skin
With puckish onslaught. Gloss they vitiate
For pure fun, when they joust through thick and thin,
Vanishes under frost, a hoar-stone slate.

Midnight, my crushed face melts in a dead heat:
Old scores ironed out, tomorrow a clean sheet.

Carlow Village Schoolhouse

Much as you need a sonnet house to save
Your muse, while sifting through our foetid pits
Of blighted roots, he needed my firm, grave
Façade, to be freed from bog-dens and sod-huts.

Such symmetry he gained from me, you got
By birth, given his names. Twenty poor scholars,
Birched if they uttered Irish words, he taught
To speak like you, faults notched on wooden collars.

We faced the crossroads four square. Where I stood
Is void now, so be fair. Not forced to sip
The cauldron soup with undying gratitude,
Would you have chosen to board a coffin-ship?

All you've seen is his proud clean signature
As a wedding witness that worst famine year.

Roof-tree

After you brought her home with your first child
How did you celebrate? Not with a poem
She might have loved, but orders to rebuild
The house. Men tore me open, room by room.

Your daughter's cries were answered by loud cracks
Of hammers stripping slates; the clawing down
Of dozed rafters; dull, stupefying knocks
On walls. Proudly your hackwork made me groan.

Your greed for kiln-dried oak that could outlast
Seven generations broke her heart. My mind
You filled with rot-proof hemlock at a cost
That killed her love. The dust spread unrefined.

To renovate my structure, which survives,
You flawed the tenderest movement of three lives.

Red Bank Restaurant

Was it a taste for black sole on the bone
Brought you two down from your mountain farm one night
To meet that Faustian guest, whose writing shone
In her sight, eating devilled prawn by candlelight?

Le sang du pauvre, he quipped, gulping more wine
You'd pay for, squandering the blood-money received
From her pilot brother's crash. Richly malign
Elevation of the hostess he'd conceived.

His cruiser eyes, when not nailed to her cross
By mother wit, fled exiled through the bar:
Soon to be reconciled, screened by clear glass,
As he smiled at his cold brilliance mirrored there.

All you could think was that your sloe hedge field
Would need spike-harrowing for a better yield.

Little Barn

It's not my place to speak more than I must
Whether of bloodstock, interest rates or corn.
She feels enclosed inside a lacquered nest
Of Chinese boxes, sealed from your concern.

I've been converted to increase the rent
Between us, cornered in a stable yard;
Spruce enclave, heavenly views; a fortress meant
To keep out southern storms; flint cobbles tarred.

Those Russian dolls her infant son and yours
Breaks open as a blue-eyed Williamite
He puts together again without more tears.
Your customs are so strange we can't unite.

She moulds the clay and fires the waterpot
He balances, authorised by you or not.

Connemara Quay

I should have done this, that and all those things
Goodwill intended when I was designed
To end the poor land's hunger. Failure brings
Catches that slip through nets too close to mind.

Men stood me up here, promising that I'd be
Their godsend: ocean would provide more food.
The green earth should have married the grey sea,
But fell foul of her storms, her moody tide.

Attached by strings of warps to my stone head,
Fine wooden craft came, to be overcome
By torpor. Keels took root in silt of seabed,
Ribbed frames rotted in a frayed hemp dream.

You played in these hulks half a century ago.
What did you think you might do? Now you know.

Birth Place

I'd been expecting death by absentee
Owner's decay, or fire from a rebel match.
Too many old relations I'd seen die
In the same bedroom made me scared to watch.

Between her cries, I heard carts trundling books
Gone mouldy to a bonfire in the yard.
Wild bees in my roof were filling up their wax
Hexagonals from our lime trees, working hard.

A boy led a pony round and round a small
Hedged pond, pumping spring water for her use.
And then your birth-cry came, piercing through wall
Behind wall. The sun transfigured all of us.

It shone like honey on doorsteps of brown bread.
The August evening kissed her worn out head.

Queen of the Castle

Her face is gone from me. Only her voice
Will spring to mind as water underground
Near an abysmal swallow-hole, the place
Where toddling after a ball you almost drowned.

A dirty rascal egged you on, then dug
His foot in your back. A giant grabbed your hair
Standing on end, with a strong gardener's tug
To root you out, and shake you in pure air.

You breathed her love away like a dandelion head
In my field of vision, looking all day long
For your duck, wandering astray. Is she dead?
Gorged by the fox? You made such a sad song.

Listen to me! She's coming back. O look!
Here, with seven ducklings. You could write a book.

Liner

I'm steaming home, ploughing your peace of mind,
With the bow-wave poise of a duchess coaching through
Her deep blue shire; buoyantly waterlined;
Brass port-holes burnished by my lascar crew.

Dolphins precede us, playing for good schools
With somersaulting skills. Petrels astern
Writhe in our screwed up wake. Obeying the rules
You're learning to spin rope quoits, turn by turn.

Child, when you've sailed half way around the world
And found that home is like a foreign country,
Think how I've had to keep an ironclad hold
On your belongings, not to lose heart at sea.

The gong is ringing. Here comes your ice cream.
There's more to mind than raising heads of steam.

Planter Stock

We're putting off the day they'll pull us down
And fell our prickly monkey-puzzle tree
That lords it over the heather in our garden
Standing up to wind and rain off the open sea.

We love the watercolours curlews paint
With iodine on a quill down a glen's throat;
Deplore the weather's poor mouth complaint;
Wear fuchsia tweed, an ancient ivy coat.

Can't you eat rabbit? Does it make you sick
To find your father's gun-shots in your meat,
Or touch a trout he's caught? You ought to like
Wearing an Eton collar; you look sweet.

All the roots that would pack inside a tea-chest
Came home when we retired from the Far East.

Family Seat

Clouds make me look as though I disapprove
Of everyone. You know that grim, grey face
Of limestone cut by famine workmen. Love
Is never allowed to show it rules the place.

But love I took from a ruling family,
And gave them back a wealth of lovely things:
As a trout river talking with propriety
Through cockshoot woods, bailiffed by underlings.

Their silver knives adored their crested forks.
Blue-veiny hands, like yours, kept my clocks wound
On endless landings: others did good works
Like typing braille. High walls surround my land.

They've all been buried in their name-proud vaults.
Paraplegics live here now, and love my faults.

Rectory

My porous rock foundations can't keep down
Rising damp from arcane rheumatic springs
That creep up walls. Wet plaster makes him frown,
As when her black dogs leap up, licking things.

She lets them loose. He's choked by a dog-collar.
Time's silver chain is hung on his clean breast.
They sniff at holy orders, flung in choler:
Scenting her cling of lavender, feel blessed.

He carpets boys like you for playing with fire.
Bitches on heat can make mixed marriages.
You're lockjawed by his chin-wag. Jubilee year,
Have you no higher thoughts than dog-rampages?

Her pups retrieve your first poem: a dead duck
Stuffed with bay leaves. Page after page they pluck.

Letterfrack Industrial School

Bog-brown glens, mica schist rocks, waterfalls
Gulching down screes, a rain-logged mountain slope
With scrawny pine trees twisted by mad gales,
They see from my ball-yard, and abandon hope.

Wild boys my workshops chasten and subdue
Learn here the force of craft. Few can escape
My rack of metal, wood, thread, hide: my screw
Of brotherhood: the penny stitched in a strap.

Podded in varnished pews, stunted in beds
Of cruciform iron, they bruise with sad, hurt shame:
Orphans with felons, bastards at loggerheads
With waifs, branded for life by a bad name.

One, almost hanged in my boot-room, has run free
Dressed as a girl, saved by a thieving gipsy.

Baymount

Describe a gate lodge like a dragon's mouth
Taking in boys and parents with a grin;
Then spitting out the parents. Iron teeth
Close when the last proud vintage car has gone.

Start counting days of terminal homesickness
Minus the love of those who left you here.
Draw six parallel lines cut quick across
Two flaming circles. Be prepared for war.

Stand up, our youngest new boy, what's-your-name!
Your uncle ate a wineglass in his mess
At Woolwich, and Dobbs major a live worm
Washed down with ink. Prove you're no cowardly ass!

Open your mouth wide, and with one bite take
The candle burning on this tower of cake!

Canterbury Cathedral

What building tuned your ear for poetry? Mine,
You remember, trained your childhood voice that filled
My quire with a sharp sound. You poured in my fine
Keyed vaults the grains of song my stonework milled.

When Canon Crum took you to climb dim stairs
That spiralled into my cranium, did you dream
You'd found my brain, with its treadmill, slow repairs,
Refacing a gargoyle, splicing an oak beam?

Now, you've come back, not to sing the *Te Deum*
In my nave, but to retrieve from your song's ground
The love you gave me then. Above the triforium
It soared to reach martyrs in stained glass crowned.

'Nine o'clock on a clear night, and all's well',
You heard as you fell asleep, with my curfew bell.

Choir School

Our mother church raised me on Kentish flint
Foundations dug in the Black Prince's day.
Two lily-white boys from dissolute Ireland,
You starred with your brother in our passion play.

How could you reach Mr Knight's perfect pitch,
Control his organ-stops, ten hands, four feet?
Good God! How could you score without a hitch
His music sheets, braced for a lofty treat?

'Glorious things' your ruff-necked voices rang
In Mr Poole's purple passage through Caen stone.
One Easter, despite Hitler's bombs, you sang
Our new Archbishop to St. Augustine's throne.

You shared my dormer view. A fiendish power
Rained fire on us: God spared Bell Harry Tower.

Suntrap

One year at home, under our flagging roof
During the war, learning and love made peace.
As with a cottage weaver's warp and woof
Your heart and mind were shuttled into place.

Verbs conjugating in our Pleasure Ground
Held the past present in contiguous time.
Here was the Bower of Bliss, painlessly scanned.
You found the oldest trees were best to climb.

In neutral Ireland, our walled demesne,
While tilting you towards knight-errant books,
Groomed you to mount on war-horses to gain
Rewards beyond our laurels, birches, oaks.

A peeled rush, dipped in tallow, carried light
From the dark ages, kissing you good night.

Gate Lodge

Two Irish yews, prickly green, poisonous,
Divide my entrance tapering in trim gloom.
Old rookery buildings, pitch-pine resinous,
Wake up shell-shocked, welcoming you back home.

Barefoot a child skips from my hearth to touch
The wrought obsequious latch of lip-service;
Taking you in, between double gates, to reach
Beyond the ruts your mother's peerless place.

I face my forebear's relic, a neat sty
That hovelled with his brogue some grateful clod
Unearthed by famine; and I hear go by
Your souper choir school voice defrauding God.

Pigeon park, pheasant wood and snipe bog lie
Within my scope: your shotgun territory.

Milford: East Wing

Stiff to open, needing a gentleman's grasp
Or a strong young maid's, my hall door, tight in its frame
Of wood at the long lime avenue's end, would gasp
With delight if callers of the old calibre came.

No judder shook my back door's ease of pulling
Lame ducks in; tinkers with babies, diseased and poor,
For a bite to eat; mockery of the cook killing
A rat with a poker on the foul scullery floor.

If it heard a piano playing, or psalms being sung,
A goat used my study door to butt in, and lie
Sniffing your mother's foot, for devilment bleating
Low notes that made your voice break on high.

My postern had to be nailed up, ivy-bound,
To keep the farmyard out of the pleasure ground.

Carlyon Bay Hotel

Designed for luxury, commandeered to house
Your bombed out school, under Spartan rule I live
In a Cornish idyll, with high and mighty views:
Royal blue channel, Phoenician tin-veined cliff.

Don't you know there's a war? It's why you're here
Debarred from girls, a pup among top dogs.
Home is ninety days off, and you've no future
Hunting hares over treacherous Irish bogs.

Wing-collared Milner scholar, don't forget
Your gas mask, ration book, identity card.
My buckthorn wood hears inklings in the blackout.
Uncle Jack's killed in Africa. Work hard!

Your voice is breaking. Kneel, and be confirmed
By Truro's hands of clay. Do you feel transformed?

Wellington College

Fear makes you lock out more than you include
By tackling my red brick with Shakespeare's form
Of love poem, barracked here and ridiculed
By hearty boys, drilled to my square-toed norm.

Yet ushered in, through my roll of honour voice,
Cold baths in winter, field days on Bagshot Heath,
Poetry gives you unconscripted choice
Of strategies, renaissance air to breathe.

Your father's brother fell in the Great War,
Your mother's fell in this. You ate our salt.
Should you plead conscience when called up next year
Their greater love would find the gravest fault.

Weren't you born to command a regiment?
How selfishly you serve your own heart's bent.

Oxford Staircase

Going up a flight of stone at seventeen
In wartime, wearing thin your plodding soles
On coupons by degrees, you pass between
Dons' billowing gowns and chapel aureoles.

Brought to your knees by genuflectory prose –
C.S. Lewis, stoking the clinkered grate
Of lost causes, keeps you on your toes –
You're taught to criticise, but not create.

That numinous cloud of jovial pipe-smoke round
His Tudor head, wraps you tongue-tied as bells
Before V.E. Day, taking steps to sound
The blissful city fraught with private hells.

A fellowship of bowls on the cloister lawn
Do you miss, old man? You slipped up, going down.

Convenience

The public servant of men's private parts,
Plain clothed in the underground below Eros,
With white glazed stalls and see-through mirror arts,
I plumb our language empire's omphalos.

Your profane oracle, I speak through a crack
In a mental block, going far back to the year
You stood here, epicentred on the shock
Of gross accusation, quaking at words like queer.

I watched you face an absurd firing squad
Unbuttoning uniforms. I, too, had lost
My primal sense in the promiscuous crowd.
Detected, blackmailed, judged, you paid the cost.

A life sentence, ambiguously imposed,
Props you behind all kinds of bars, exposed.

Lecknavarna

Look where I'm stuck the wrong side of Lough Fee:
Bad road, no neighbours, in the squally shade
Of a bleak mountain. Yet you took to me
When young. What made you seek my solitude?

Did you need my poor virgin concrete shell
No family cared to live in, just to write
Poetry, worshipping my waterfall,
Abased in loneliness by lust at night?

Still flowing steadfast in a flagstone cleft
Of stunted alders clinging on, it pours
With resonant gravity, bringing the gift
Of widespread raindrops crafted to great force.

Hearing that strong cadence, you learned your trade
Concerned with song in endless falling, stayed.

Killary Hostel

The young have redressed my slated history
Nailed to this wild coast in the famished past
On a deep ocean inlet, and restored me
As their last outpost of folksong and feast.

Mackerel swim through my windows at high tide.
You blotted a blank page of lyrical youth
With epic faults in my loneliest interlude,
Hooked here in boyhood on the Tir na nÓg myth.

Didn't you follow that exiled Austrian
Who stood on my murky lane with a walking-stick
Drawing diagrams for the birds to explain?
Sea-urchins mocked him with folkloric tricks.

He left, in my turf-shed rafters, a small sign
To question all our myths... *Dear Wittgenstein.*

Waterkeeper's Bothy

My deeds are tied up in a family trust
Embracing a salmon river, nightly poached
By sweep-nets, to her ladyship's disgust,
Her private reaches tortuously encroached.

Tucked behind rhododendron palisades
I sheathe you with your mate in a dug-out gloom.
You lumber home at dawn to cast-iron beds,
Trickle of spawn-tanks through a shuttered room.

I'm living in the past, among record fish
She hooked on badger-hair, played to her gaff,
Carved for blue-blooded guests on a Ming dish
And immortalised with a game book epitaph.

While watching, do you poach? With sovereign guile
Beyond reproach, she only kills in style.

Kylemore Castle

Built for a cotton king, who loved the view
Unspoilt by mills, improved by famine's hand
That cleared away people, petrified I grew
Grotesquely rich on mountainous, poor land.

To last for ever, I had to be faced in stone
Dressed by wage-skeletons; a spindly pile
Of storm-grey turrets that defended no one,
And broke my maker, with his fabricated style.

Coming from church to hold her usual place
On Christmas nights, wheeled to the dining-room,
His wife's corpse embalmed in a sealed glass case
Obeyed his command in the brandy-lit gloom.

Now, my linen-fold panelled halls retain
In mortmain his dark airs, which nuns maintain.

Tony White's Cottage

Never to be finished was the work he'd planned
When he restored my site, rebuilt the wreck
Of burnt thatch and disbonded walls he'd found
Bleak on a hillock between the ocean and a lake.

A weird huckster had lodged here in the past
Who could cure all diseases; he used to talk
To a dark rock split by lightning; the last
Night he walked out there he never came back.

Always your friend looked forward to being alone
In my raw stone skin, with a wren and a mouse
That crept through random masonry, while a swan
Nested on an island he saw through raindrop glass.

Never to be finished was the life you'd planned
To spend near him. How well he'd understand!

Pier Bar

For donkey's years I've stood in lashing rain
Unbudgingly, casting a fish-hawk eye
On dock-tied hookers. How could we regain
Lost native custom tourist cash would buy?

Snug in my torporific trammelled air
Of a dream village roped to a lifeless quay,
I can help you play with an old craft, but your
Ten-feathered jigs will get fouled up at sea.

What brings you back to me, having said goodbye
To bull-head shillings in my hand-carved till,
Unless to greet, reflected through my dry
Distillery, the dead friend whose glass I fill?

Why drown so carefully with moss-hung chain
On sound moorings? Rig me. I'll entertain.

Miners' Hut

Unused in your desk drawer lies my brass key
To tongue-tied stonework, musky fossil tunes
You've locked away. Come back, not to unmask me
Word for word, but to make me sound in my ruins.

I rose from a desecration of corbelled cells
And hermits' graves in a walled sanctuary:
Rock taken over by great black-backed gulls
Saluting each other *Sieg Heil*, claiming the sky.

Sink no more mineshafts to bring up fool's gold
With fever. You can't give every spall's lost face
A niche in the anchoretic oratory. Hold
My still-room as a rock-pipit's nesting place.

Bring oil to unseize my lock. The lode of ore
To smelt will sound like a fault: wheatear, shearwater.

Hexagon

Three watchful openings of clear plate glass
Give you command of a stormy desolate view
From my hilltop sundial cell as you look across
Dunes, rocks and sea to islands west of Omey.

Six random walls round one all-purpose room
Of calm rupestral concentricity,
With a smell of yeast-bread flowering, enwomb
Your pride in the hermit hut you made of me.

Oak bed, a hundred books, a staunch teak door
And the Twelve Pins of your childhood I include.
No need for you to write. Sun and moon pore
Over curled up fly-leaves, brilliantly intrude.

Flood-tide, closing the strand, comes to embrace
Our isolation. Blue arms interlace.

New Forge

From derelict huts of Cleggan rock I grew
To look most natural here, though I began
Strangely; your Breton stone design drawn through
A London architect's Dunfermline plan.

For thirteen years this perfect place to write
Creviced you in my Galway garden bond;
Green Cumbrian slates letting in attic light;
Slieve Donard heather's white cross-border stand.

Why did you sell me? Did you feel trapped here,
Compelled in cold blood to exuviate
My hard pink shell? A Dublin auctioneer
Hammered you free to grow articulate.

Our union was split level. Now I'm used
To keep old men with infant minds amused.

Cottage for Sale

If you have lost someone you tried to own
Buy me instead. I need to be possessed
For more than seaside weekends: stone by stone
Personified, gaps filled with interest.

Build on my real estate; squander in style
Your passion for belongings; ditch your thought.
Restore old thatch, strip off asbestos tile.
Shape me with love I can't escape, being bought.

Bring children here, and spoil them with my view
Of ocean; burnet roses growing between
Granite outcrops. Let barbed wire renew
Your land bonds. Plant me with a windproof screen.

I'm on the market. Hear my brochure's cry:
Vacant possession, sewn up endlessly.

Horse-drawn Caravan

My red half-door opens. The mother of nine
Looks at the tip-head where we've stuck, and curses.
'Whenever he took us out of one misfortune
He brought us into another that was worse.'

How many stitches I got, sheltering those two
With their hatchets! They'd slash the skewbald cob
To tread down gaps in hedges we'd go through.
Mostly it was each other's joy they'd rob.

I'd rock like a cradle when they'd start to brawl
Over bottles. Storms did less harm than the pair of them
Spigoting my barrel-top. No luck at all,
No calm until cuckoo slipped into Jerusalem.

If I'm not scrapped sooner, or sold for the price
Of a drink, she'll burn me when the old lad dies.

Old Dispensary

A horse trotting loose, or a cow might stray
By my comatose door. Nobody passed a remark,
All the years I desquamated in decay
Tumorous on the bog-road in the priestly dark.

Now there's a new earth-mover's claw to feed,
The jaws are chewing me over. Neighbours are scared
Because they've heard I'll house a lazy breed
Of verminous, ditch-born tinkers, if repaired.

Let them come, with banners of torn teeshirts hung
From smashed windows, looks that will turn the milk
Of decent mothers sour. Let my stone sing
With tongues of cant. Let the saintly village sulk.

How can they move me if I keep folk bound
Like spavined jennets padlocked in the pound?

Chalet

No shelter on this site when ocean gales
Assault my cabbage-green school weatherboards:
I stand rebuilt on ground made up of shells,
Dock silt and worms, clay pipes and bog orchids.

Nuns moved me here to install itinerants
With seven children, lost at a district court,
Dumped for their parents' fault in stone-walled convents.
My joinery cramped the family it restored.

Makeshift immobile home, need I be stilted,
Unstable? When my aerial blows down
They kick holes in my roof of mineral felt;
Beg to be changed to a multi-channel town.

Tears, temper, screams, my battered frame endures
By dint of carpentry, no miracle cures.

Prison

Losing your pen in the body-search behind
My dustbin-columned classical façade,
You're led by intercrural routes to find
Your gipsy friend, trussed in my fixed abode.

Before he lost his capricious boyhood, grew
A centaur's beard, hooves, haunches in relief,
Did you cage him with hubristic love? You knew
His touching thievery often gave you life.

Free to face across doubly screened zoo wire,
Stop-watched by warders in a cell, you meet,
Deterred by a faecal smell, beyond desire
Where words fail to regenerate, but cheat.

Poor old people he robbed in bed at night.
What sentence did your teaching help him write?

Wattle Tent

Lobawn, he calls me in shelta, his duck nest
Under a thorn-bush on a petering out lane;
Wattled with hazel cut from the remotest
Copse of a departed ascendancy demesne.

Fourteen lithe rods, carved into wishbones, keep
My head up in the rain. My tarred and buttered
Skin he's smoked and cured. Rats from a trash-heap
Steal bits of his begged bread, but he's not bothered.

Thrown back by cheap wine on to his last straw
He finds I can help the pain. His seed has spread
From road to road: boys gathering scrap in new
Pick-ups, girls as young as Juliet wedded.

It dawns on me, when his bantam cock crows,
I'll house him till he dies, wherever he goes.

Newgrange

Brought to a brumal standstill, here I lie
Obliquely floored, mouth curbed by stones that speak
In pick-dressed spirals, egghead sucked bone dry,
Waiting for dawn inside my skull to streak.

Sungod and riverbride died in my bed
To live as bead and elkshorn under earth.
One cairn eye stayed open to feed the dead
A ray of wintry hope, fixed on rebirth.

Up a dark passage, brightening from far back,
A sunbeam seeks my carved leakproof abode.
As pollen dust ignites my pebble stack
The tomb I've made becomes a vivid road.

Once a year it may strike me, a pure gift
Making light work, a mound of greywacke lift.

Friary

Each time you breathe my name – Ross Errilly –
Young leaf-growth rustles in the druid wood,
Felled to convert my land so thoroughly
Stone crosses stand on grass where forest stood.

Here the rain harps on ruins, plucking lost
Tunes from my structure, which the wind pours through
In jackdaw desecration, carping at the dust
And leprous sores my towers like beggars show.

Now my fish ponds hold no water. Doors and aisles
Are stacked with donors' tombs, badly invested,
A gift for peeping toms: my lecherous gargoyles
Hacked off by thieves, the bones unresurrected.

Here, too, buried in rhyme, lovers lie dead,
Engraved in words that live each time they're read.

Beehive Cell

There's no comfort inside me, only a small
Hart's-tongue sprouting square, with pyramidal headroom
For one man alone kneeling down: a smell
Of peregrine mutes and eremitical boredom.

Once, in my thirteen hundred years on this barren
Island, have I felt a woman giving birth,
On her own in my spinal cerebellic souterrain,
To a living child, as she knelt on earth.

She crawled under my lintel that purgatorial night
Her menfolk marooned her out of their coracle
To pick dillisk and sloke. What hand brought a light
With angelica root for the pain of her miracle?

Three days she throve in me, suckling the child,
Doing all she had to do, the sea going wild.

Natural Son

Before the spectacled professor snipped
The cord, I heard your birth-cry flood the ward,
And lowered your mother's tortured head, and wept.
The house you'd left would need to be restored.

No worse pain could be borne, to bear the joy
Of seeing you come in a slow dive from the womb,
Pushed from your fluid home, pronounced 'a boy'.
You'll never find so well equipped a room.

No house we build could hope to satisfy
Every small need, now that you've made this move
To share our loneliness, much as we try
Our vocal skill to wall you round with love.

This day you crave so little, we so much
For you to live, who need our merest touch.

PART SIX

Sri Lanka

and poems finished in the years
1985-2012

Mangoes

I

A colourful boy in a Star Wars tee-shirt
and a saffron batik sarong
tightrope walking along a mango tree's
top branches
figurine fired in the midday sun
is raining down on the parched red earth
glittering hard green fruit.

Seeing you focus binoculars
to pick him out
as a black-headed oriole of Ceylon
for your notebook's cage
he shins down the trunk embracingly
to bring you a gift of mangoes robbed
with a tartly negotiable smile.

II

Where are you going? A terracotta road
   Winds from a tower-block on a tourist beach
   Around a lake dyed bottle-green with garbage
Of a foetid shanty slum. It turns your head.
Out of the ditch a pearly grinning guide
   With Tamil pride in his bold English speech
   Springs up to fasten on you, like a leech,
Charm that could make your skin feel deified.

You can hide nothing on this scathing track
   Which puts on trial your childhood. You are lost
   For want of a poor abandoned native boy
To love and father, giving him the luck
   Showered on you here in your imperial past
   With soaring confidence, great guilt, much joy.

National Hero

Couched in cement and whitewash at my feet
Four lions cast a monumental grin
On cricket pitch, kovil and minaret,
Bo tree with beggars cringing from the sun.

High on the clashing horns of trishaw, van,
Minibus, juggernaut, I'm equipoised,
Reborn in bronze, a Singhalese businessman
Who died in the king's uniform disgraced.

'Shot as a lesson for all traitors to come,'
The Town Guard captain who refused to shoot
Rioters of my own race, I feel calm
Redressed in loyalty buttoned to the throat.

Going up a martyr's moonstone steps to power
When mobs loot, burn and slaughter, I inspire.

Colombo, 1985

Sigiriya

11 January 1987

Early this morning
    I walked on the ramparts
        And came across lotuses,

A playful flotilla
    becalmed on the moat
        hauling white sails down,

As warm rain was falling:
    each leaf collecting in the palm
        of my hand as a child

Drops that scatter and split
    like mercury: held very still
        they pool and unite.

                                           *

We were lightly fanned
    by a friendly wind
        with a scent of jasmine

Around an octagonal pond
    where the king could recline
        in his pleasure ground

Backed by a red rock lingam
    watering a lotus bed
        whenever it rained:

We could see our reflections
    blossoming from the mud
        in fragrant, flamboyant air.

                                         *

The freshness we found
   near the cobra hood cave
      on white marble steps

Going up to the clouds
   came as kindness from someone
      who makes our blood boil:

All the better when we stood
   on the gallery walkway
      between rock and mirror wall,

And watched a transparent
   drop-curtain of rain
      coming down from the gods

By drip-channels grooved
   in the overhanging cliff:
      and saw the violent green

Jungle of the country
   from this high point of love
      diffused through a purifying screen.

Sri Lanka

Being nearly heart-shaped made me seem a ham
    On early spice trade navigators' charts
    Tinctured with cinnamon, peppered with forts,
To be eaten up under a strong brand name
Like Taprobane, Serendip, Tenarisim –
    Copper-palmed lotus island slave resorts –
    And I succumbed to lordly polished arts
That cut me down to seem a white king's gem,
A star sapphire teardrop India shed
    On old school maps, a lighthouse of retorts
Flashing from head to head. My leonine blood
Throbbed wildly when resplendent freedom came
    Mouthing pearl tropes with Pali counterparts,
Exalted, flawed; and made me seem as I am.

National Tree

The flowers of the ironwood
Last for a day.
Opening at sunrise
They fall when the sun goes down.

Their little white flags
With yellow hearts
Flutter in a state
Of carnival and terror.

Yesterday's petals
Lie beheaded on the ground.
There are buds in hiding:
Tomorrow these will explode.

Above the low scrub jungle
Seething in hot air
The young leaves turn
Transparently blood-red.

A king cobra demon
Stays hoodwinking on top.
The ironwood grows high
Exuding festivity.

Kandy, January 1989

Death in Kandy

New Year's Day, 1990,
Between midnight and dawn
At the Olde Empire Hotel
Drums from the Tooth Relic Temple
Are keeping me awake.
Anura, my friend,
Has been made to disappear.
Military intelligence has warned me
Not to interfere, because
'Anura is non-existent.'

Dragged by soldiers from door
To door through five villages,
Stripped to the waist, bleeding
From head to foot,
Hands tied behind his back,
Exposed as a terrorist,
Unable to prove his innocence,
Unable to talk with smashed teeth,
Anura was told,
'Your friend can't help you now!'

On a bend where drivers park
To show tourists the Mahaweli
River that borders the former
Great University of Ceylon
I saw a skeleton
Picked clean by dogs and crows,
A nameless victim like Anura
Stretched on a burnt-out tyre
Under the vertical sun
Of smiling resplendent Sri Lanka.

A River of Notebooks

In a river of notebooks
Under the bridge of my desk
I fish for poems in pools of words
That for half a century
Have flowed from my pen
Gathering less poetry than sludge.
Often I snag
On corroded bars of domestic argument
And effortful literary debris.
Trout on a calm sunny day
Won't rise to a fly
Or swallow a worm on a hook.
A breeze has to animate the surface
And mystify the deep
To bring a reward after years of my
Winkling through dictionaries for bait.
Poetry feeds on the refuse of time
Against whose current it swims.

Double Vision

A half-ripe cataract in my left eye
          makes the world
     look like a damaged old master

My right eye has a view
         of unvarnished clarity
     through a new synthetic lens

At night my left eye
         sees the numinous
     glory of the moon blurred

My right eye pictures it
         hanging from a parachute
     by miniscule threads of light

Rite of Passage

When he steals into my body's old temple
My subversive lover stands
For a minute of silence
Before his dance of death begins
With the beating of drums
Followed by the stillness of a lotus on a pond
And the sound of a woodpecker tapping on a tree.

Avatar of youth that has passed me by,
Devil dancer who expels with a flaming brand
The troubles that plague me,
Healer, whose fingertips
Regenerate my fabric of decay,
He comes with tom-toms loud as thunder
Exploding across a river that has burst its banks.

Prostrate among the ruins of his making
He reclines in the forever of my love
As a lotus planted in memory,
Till the ringing of a cell phone
Calls him away
Leaving me drenched
In his dark aroma of godlike indifference.

Waking from a Dream

All night the sea rose from the distant past
And flushed the brackish pools on the pebbled shore
Of memory. I fished in the long lost
Years of Armada wrecks hugging their store
Of plundered gold, and as I wished the more
Embattled the waves flashed
And the moon rose
Astonished from the pillows on a bed of cloud.

Vagrant

Who is tapping on my study window
At this late hour tonight

Disturbing the calm yellow pool
Of light on the unfinished page?

If only it were the fingers
Of one who will never come home.

Draw back the curtain
And look your loneliness in the eyes:

Wind is thrashing on the glass
The scarlet hips of a rose.

Last Word

Her voice is a mist on the phone
Far away and precarious
As a tree whose roots cling
To rock overhanging a cliff
As she threatens to hang up.

Years pass into dust
With drills, hammers and saws
Remodelling an old house
Whose walls of silence
Keep a granite hold on my loss.

Now that she'll never intrude
On my rock garden concord
Far away through a static mist
I hear in her voice
Endless silence falling dead.

APPENDIX

Author's note on the provenance of 'Sailing to an Island'

During the summer of 1952, to support myself while trying to finish an obscurely mythological mini-epic called 'Voyage to an Island', I took a night job as a water-bailiff guarding salmon from poachers along eight miles of the Eriff River in County Mayo. The job was like living in a poem, but far too long; it left little incentive though plenty of time to write. When it rained heavily, the salmon were safe, as the current became too strong for the poachers' nets. So my employer, Alice Marsh, allowed me to go away for a day or two.

My older brother Chris, on leave from his job in London, had hired, with its young owner, Padraic O Maille of Ballyconneely, an old sailing boat of a local design known as a pookaun (Irish: 'púcán) – 'pretty to look at but dangerous', according to a quote in *The Oxford English Dictionary*. This pookaun had a bad reputation. Five men had been lost out of her in the Cleggan disaster of 1927, the year I was born. Her owner – the future father of the poet Mary O'Malley – was too poor to buy timber, so he had sealed her leaking bilge with cement that acted as ballast. He had rigged her, not as a pookhaun with a single dipping lugsail, but with a gaff-rigged mainsail, a boom and a foresail.

So, on the 25th August 1952, my brother and I set out, with our nine-year-old nephew, John Caulfeild, and my employer's daughter, Alison, a talented sculptor, as passengers, from the quay of Rosroe near the mouth of the Big Killary harbour. We were planning to go to Clare Island, a place renowned for legends. We never got there. Contrary winds brought us instead to an island I had never heard of, called Inishbofin.

A week later, alone in the pre-famine Coast Guard cottage on the quay at Rosroe, I wrote the first draft of a poem about our rough passage and change of course that led to a change in my life. My mini-epic died of natural causes; but after some fortuitous redirections, including marriage and divorce, through Crete, Brittany, Wicklow, London, and back to Inishbofin in 1959, the poem I had drafted at Rosroe, revised and revised, emerged in 1963 as the final version of 'Sailing to an Island'.

The provenance of 'Wittgenstein and the Birds'

Tommy Mulkerrins, caretaker of the Quay House at Rosroe, which I was renting for £20 a year in 1951 after winning the Æ Memorial Award for Poetry, thought I must be lonely living on my own.

'It's a pity you weren't here two years ago,' he said, 'you'd have enjoyed talking to the man who was staying here then, a friend of Con Drury, Myles's brother.'

'Who was that?'

'I have his name written down at home but could never get my tongue around it. He was a German translator of sorts. Con had met him at Cambridge and brought him here for holidays before the war. He told Con to take up medicine, so Con became a psychiatrist in Dublin. The man was here by himself for several months in 1949. He wasn't well.'

'What was he doing at Rosroe?'

'He was writing all the time like you. After he'd written a whole pile of pages he'd tell me to burn them.'

'Did you?' I asked.

'Of course. What use would they be except to light fires?'

Another day Tommy told me, 'Your man was fond of walking, but he'd not be gone more than a hundred yards up the road before he'd stop and stand for twenty minutes, drawing signs with his walking stick in the gravel.'

One day at lunch in the kitchen Tommy pointed to the table and said, 'I seen a robin coming in and eating off this table. Your man was like St Francis with the birds on his shoulders and his hands. He was so keen to watch sea birds that he asked me to build him a hut on Inishbarna.'

'Did you do this?'

'No, because, you see, if I'd built him a hut on the island, he'd have wanted me to be carrying down the curragh on my back to the shore and rowing him out there every day. We might have been caught in a storm. He asked would I let him sleep in my house, but I said no. There was only my bed he could have slept in. He had cases of baked beans sent up on the bus from Lipton's in Galway. A middling poor man, he was, who had once been rich. He told me he'd given all his money away because he didn't want to be wealthy. I'd like to have met him before he gave it away.

He wasn't bad, mind you. When he was leaving he gave me some money to buy food for the birds in the garden.'

'Did you do this?'

'Not for long. He had those birds so tame that the cats ate them.'

When I had visitors in August, among them Charles Monteith, a young editor at Faber and Faber, I moved out of the Quay House to sleep in the turf shed. Lying in bed looking up at the rafters supporting rusty corrugated iron sheets, I noticed a wedge of blue paper folded between a rafter and the iron to stop it rattling. I took down the wedge and found two letters that I showed to Charles, one beginning 'My dear Ludwig' and the other 'Dear Professor Wittgenstein'.

That name, a mystery to me, meant 'everything that is the case' to Charles, who used to dine with philosophers every weekend at All Souls. He informed me that Wittgenstein had published only one book in his life, but notes taken by disciples at his lectures had been passed from hand to hand like gospels. It was only four months since the great man had died of cancer. Tommy must have burnt the worksheets of a book Wittgenstein was trying to finish. Charles quoted, 'Death is not an event in life: it is not lived through.'

from *The Kick: A Life Among Writers* (Lilliput Press e-book)

Author's note on 'The Last Galway Hooker'

After my divorce from Patricia Avis in London, I returned to Inishbofin in 1959 and bought a boat that many men had loved. I fell in love with her and lived on her for a while, fishing by day and sleeping in her cabin at night. Built by Seán Cloherty of Inishnee and his daughter in 1922 on Long Wall, across the Corrib river from the Claddagh, the *Ave Maria* was the last hooker to be built for a fisherman in Galway.

In the eighteenth and nineteenth centuries there were perhaps five hundred hookers in the Claddagh fleet. Here the word 'hooker' may have been derived from the Dutch 'hoeker', a fishing vessel that had plied off the west coast of Ireland for centuries. The superstition that used to bar women from having anything to do with boats was flouted in her building. A woman had planked her. The *Ave Maria* was larger than a pookaun – 32 feet from stem to stern, with a single mast, a gaff-rigged mainsail, a foresail and a jib. Much abused by foul weather, she appealed to me because she looked old and in need of renewal.

Photographs of Inishbofin – May 1960

A dialogue between two boatmen

Me and Murphy put the new white sails on the *Ave Maria* beyond in the hole. Mainsail, foresail and jib. First tack, down the mouth of Glassilaun. Out by the current.

Down the mouth. Out by the current.

Murphy before the mast. Change the foresail.

Change the foresail.

My John went back in the pookhaun. Beating her over the harbour he was. First tack across to Porth.

Across to Porth.

I seen the Dublin man from the Tourist Board running from Dooneen with his camera to the edge of the quay. Putting Inishofin on the map.

Bofin on the map. Where it never was before.

Murphy'd spent a fortune turning Scuffle's half-rotten hooker into a yacht. Not one bit afraid of drowning himself and his crew. You'd find no holy pictures in *his* engine-room. That man put his faith in a shagging liferaft.

A shagging life-raft! Must have been idle rich.

Sure he was rotten with money, but what did he know about sailing? Never been out in a storm in his life. Sunshine fisherman. Still, he wanted to take the tiller from me to show the whole world he could sail.

You wouldn't give the tiller to a man like that?

I gave him the tiller. Says I, 'Sail her now, Murphy, if you're able!' I went up before the mast. Across to the corner of the quay from Porth he brought the boat.

Fair enough.

Listen! He takes her over the current and across the hole. God knows how he missed ramming the small boats moored there. Puts her about, catches more wind. Then down the mouth he lets her fly – the jackass! – tiller hard over, going straight for the quay.

Dear God! Straight for the quay. Heaven help you!

Murphy shouted to me, 'What will I do now, Pat?', and I was before the mast. 'Do what you like with her now,' says I, 'she's your boat. I thought you told me you knew how to sail.' He couldn't handle her. 'Here!' I shouted, 'come out of that cockpit you mad greenhorn and give me the tiller.' I took the tiller. Blessed myself. Still he wasn't satisfied. Wanted more photographs.

More photographs! Working the head, he was, bringing tourists to Bofin. No better man. Plenty of porter for everyone in Micho's. Good luck to him!

'Pat,' he says in his English voice, real polite, 'please bring her round again by Glassilaun.' Up the mouth this time and into the hole we run, before turning back, beyond the moorings of the *Topaz*. Then down the mouth again, lying on her side, three sails full. The sea boiling over her deck. Surely the grandest picture a cameraman could find. And do you know what Murphy wanted me to do next?

What more could you do?

Wanted me to take her over the current from the mouth, let down sail, and turn her in sharp for the quay. What no man ever did in his born life!

Heavenly Lord! What did he know about boats except to sink them?

Published in *Poetry Ireland Review* 37 (Winter '92/'93), edited by Peter Denman, and in *Poetry Ireland Review* 50 (1996), edited by Michael Longley.

A note on the provenance of 'The Cleggan Disaster'

I returned from London to Rosroe in May 1953, went by mailboat from Cleggan to Inishbofin, and bought a pookaun from Pat Concannon, who had been among the 'whispering spontaneous reception committee' I had met on the quay as described in 'Sailing to an Island'. We sailed the pookaun to Rosroe on a Sunday, taking seven hours to reach the quay. On our journey Pat was teaching me how to manage a pookaun single-handed, and telling me more about his struggle to survive the great storm of 1927 with four other men at sea on a winter's night in a boat the same size as the pookaun. Here, in his own words, arranged for continuity, is Pat Concannon's story, the source of my poem, 'The Cleggan Disaster,' which would take me another eight years and a much longer visit to the island to write.

'I could be a month telling you what happened on that night, and I wouldn't have a tenth told, not in years if I was to tell all I went through in those eight hours fighting the waves. It was pure calm when we went out after dark. The last meal we had about four o'clock. We had no food in the boat. We never brought food in the boat.

'I was up in the stem of the boat, my knees under the gunwale, holding the rope, keeping her head up over the wave, facing the storm, now this way, now that. Sometimes the wave would break right on top of me. I had the worst of it. I told the others to row, give them something to do. We could do nothing only keep her head into the storm. They were three young lads. There was one older man, but he was no seaman. We believed we were lost. My hands were skinned with the ropes. When she went down in the trough I had to pull in, and when she went up on the crest I had to give her more rope: otherwise the nets would have pulled the stem under the big wave, or she'd have been turned broadside onto the storm.

'They say I'm a good boatsman. What do they mean? They know nothing about boats at all. Now *he* was a good boatsman, Michael O'Toole, my brother-in-law. His skull was broken at Derryinver. And he was a good boatsman, Patrick Powell. His boat was upset, and came towards us in the storm, so close that I had to put my foot on the upturned keel to fend it off, and maybe he was trapped inside. When one of the lads heard his own brother crying for help in the water, he caught him by the hand, but the hand slipped from his grasp and sank under the boat. My cousin who slept in the same bed with me was lost in O'Toole's boat. He was a great swimmer, could lie on the water for hours. The waves smothered him.

'I thought of my mother and the girl I was courting at the time. We had known one another a long time. That's all right, that's love. I married her two years after. I thought all the time of God. We were saying our prayers. Acts of contrition. Love God because he is good and for Himself only, and go straight to heaven. You mustn't be afraid of hell. That's no good. Some of them shat in their pants. Frightened? Weren't we all frightened?

'That was the hardest test any man could have in his life, what I went through, to hold onto those nets all night and not to give up with the waves breaking in my face and on my chest all the time. The nets saved us because the ebbtide dragged them against the storm away out far from the shore. I couldn't see at all, blinded with spray. My hands were skinned to the bone holding the rope that held the nets, we call it the guide rope. If she went across on the heave she was lost, I had to keep her bows into it all the time, pulling her this way, then that, to face the storm. No talk at all on the boat, all I said was law, only keep the boat bailed. No oars out. Pull her up to meet the sea, keep working the rope in the stem all the time.

'Around Lyon Head, under the light, we were dragged close to Carraig-mahog, and a big wave shot up like an arm from the sea to put out the light. But though it has failed us these fifteen years, it kept its flame all that night. We were heading for High Island when the tide turned at the Cuddoo Rocks, and we cut our nets, cut them all away there, at 2 a.m., put out the oars and rowed.

'We rowed for about an hour, rowing backwards all the time to keep her facing the storm. We crossed a breaker. Then we saw land which Billy Lavelle recognised as Dog Island. We were in the calm then, we knew where we were. We opened the bay of Cleggan and rowed straight to the quay.

'There was no one on the quay when we landed, and the five of us in our wet clothes walked straight up the main street to Stephen King's shop. They led me by the hand because the spray had made my eyes swell up and blinded me. It was about three o'clock, and the skin was torn off the palms of my hands. The first person we met in the shop was Stephen's sister, and I said, 'Hullo, Bridget, what's keeping you up so late this night?' and she said, 'Is that you, Pat, God bless you, what brought you to Cleggan?' and I said, 'I had a message to bring over.' With so many lost on the beaches, it was hard to believe we had landed safely.

'We rowed into the East End the next day. Everyone came down to the shore meeting us. Michael Schofield' – Pat pronounced his name 'Scuffle' – 'came back from Dawros later. A man from his boat was seen the next day wandering through a field carrying a bailer. In Darcy's boat they bailed all night with their boots.

'What can I say of such a hard night now? I'm alive myself. Good men are gone. When a man doesn't know what to do, he does what he can, and he may do wrong. I'm getting old. I wish I had half the strength to use again. Boats are rotting on the beaches around here. The boys won't go out. With their backs to the wall, they scratch themselves like donkeys, but more idle. It's easy for them to manage on the dole. We weren't paid for doing nothing then. We had to fish. Don't mind the weather, it was live on seaweed, or go out. Often it was both, we had so little to eat. That was better than eating too much.

'Willie Burke's father could build a pookaun in nine days. Willie took three weeks to build a pookaun himself. His son isn't able to build a pookaun at all. There may be more money now, but I'd sooner be young and have my strength again whatever the hardship. It's worse to be old than hungry. There were more fish in those days and more men to go fishing. Lobsters were half a crown a dozen, and all we got for mackerel was five shillings a hundred. What good is money to a man that drinks it?

'It isn't only yourself you have to think of, going out in a boat, if you're lost: there's your mother at home, and you'd be afraid for her sake more than your own. Write nothing about the dead. Their people wouldn't like it. The bodies weren't found.

'What is it all anyway but your luck? If your time is up then you'll have to go.'

Adapted from *The Kick: A Life Among Writers* (Lilliput Press e-book)

THE BATTLE OF AUGHRIM

In August 1968 the BBC Third Programme twice broadcast the poem in a reading by C. Day Lewis, Ted Hughes, Cyril Cusack, Niall Toibín and Margaret Robertson, with music by Seán Ó Riada and his group Ceoltóirí Chualann. A recording of this is available on CD from Claddagh Records.

In October 1968 RTE broadcast a film version of the poem, read by Siobhan McKenna and Richard Murphy, with music by Seán Ó Riada at the harpsichord. Directed by Jack Dowling, this film was RTE's entry for the Golden Harp Award.

Writing *The Battle of Aughrim*

I started writing *The Battle of Aughrim* in the 'disaster' village of Cleggan on the morning of the second Sunday in July 1962. I was alone in Mary Concannon Coyne's unmodernised thatched cottage for an hour while she and her family and most people were away at Mass. My nearby cottage was let to a British family that had chartered one of my two hookers, the *True Light*. Mary's red half-door was open towards the Diamond mountain in the east. There was not a sound in the calm but a little squabbling of chickens under a hedge and the lowing of a distant cow. The previous day had ended with me kneeling down with the family while Mary recited the Rosary.

Thinking of this, and the fanfare of Orange marches in the North to celebrate victories of 1690 and 1691 that had dispossessed the Irish Catholics, I remembered driving through the village of Aughrim, right in the centre of Ireland, and feeling a sense of desolation in the place. The battle fought there on Sunday, the 12th July 1691, was the last and bloodiest in a war that established the Protestant ownership of land in Ireland for almost the next two centuries. The famine of 1845-1847, the partitioning of Ireland in 1922, and the long ebb tide of emigration that was, we hoped, about to turn, were remote consequences of the battle. And I recalled that one of my mother's ancestors, Robert Miller, had acquired from a dispossessed

Catholic the land and house he called Milford, where I was born.

A question uppermost in all Irish minds in our agricultural past – *who owns the land?* – occurred to me so strongly that I took an envelope from the pocket of my donkey jacket and wrote those words, in case I might forget them during a day of chatting to tourists while trying to navigate safely to and from Inishbofin on the *Ave Maria*. One written word led to another, with crossings out, more or less in this rough form:

Who owns the land where musket balls are buried
Under whitethorns on the esker, in the drained bogs
Where flocks of sheep browse and redcoats waded?

From then on, I became curious to learn 'exactly what took place, what it could mean.' I had written enough externally about boats and the sea in *Sailing to an Island*. Now I wanted to look inward at the divisions and devastations in myself as well as in Ireland: the conflicts, legends, rituals, myths and histories arising from possession of the land – why we still had borders and bigotries.

At a meeting of the Military History Society at Renmore Barracks in Galway, I met Professor Hayes McCoy and Martin Joyce, the National Teacher at Aughrim. Martin presented me with a musket ball from the battlefield, and later invited me to stay at his house so that he could escort me round the battlefield describing what happened in the present tense as if it were happening now. He had a museum of objects relating to the battle in his school, and he lived in two time zones, the present and the 12th July 1691.

The BBC Third Programme was a good patron of poets in the Sixties, with the novelist P.H. Newby as director, and Douglas Cleverdon able to commission whatever he liked after his success with Dylan Thomas's *Under Milk Wood*. Douglas had recently produced a reading by Denys Hawthorne of *The Cleggan Disaster* that was well rated by Audience Research in the BBC; and when I told him my thoughts about Aughrim, he commissioned me to write a poem long enough to fill a programme lasting one hour, of which fifteen minutes could be music. The fee was small – the price of *The Oxford English Dictionary* in its original twelve volumes – but the value of knowing that the poem would have an audience was great. I never thought it would take me over five years to fulfil the contract, or that Douglas would be so patient.

By good fortune I had met Seán Ó Riada a few months earlier, at a poetry reading I gave at the National Book League in London. He had come in a white Aran sweater that matched the one I was wearing, knitted by Mary Coyne. My impression was of a man of immense charm and panache, who enhanced everything he said and did with a touch of comedy and heroism. The moguls of the film industry were trying to hire him as a composer, but his passion to revive Irish folk music in a modern form was keeping him in Ireland, where we both were to travel a few nights later.

We met at Euston station on the Irish mail train bound for Holyhead. As I was travelling third class, Seán invited me to join him for a drink in the first class sleeping car. There he introduced me to what he called 'wedges' – a pint of Guinness followed by a shot of rum or whiskey followed by another pint of Guinness – more than I could handle; and he invited me to come to his house in Dublin some night to hear him rehearse a group of traditional musicians who spoke Irish.

His house was on Galloping Green in Stillorgan, and his group was known as Ceoltóirí Chualann – out of which would emerge The Chieftains. The sound of the uilleann pipes, a goatskin drum, a flute, a penny whistle and two fiddles, with the verve that Seán brought out in six Dubliners, most of whom had done a hard day's work in an office or on a bus, enchanted me as if it were coming from the ground out of a hawthorn-ringed rath, bringing the music of the dead to life with renewed vitality.

The music was oral, made up at rehearsals and not written down. Spontaneity was in vogue in the London theatre, a breakthrough from the Old Vic and all rigidities of Shakespearean actors. Joan Littlewood had encouraged her cast at Stratford in East London to improve Brendan Behan's play *The Hostage* by extemporising. Ó Riada's group was at once spontaneous and archaic, wringing from the past a passionate sound that ranged with pathos and humour through all the emotions from grief to joy.

After this rehearsal we talked about my idea of a long poem on the theme of the Battle of Aughrim, and I asked Seán to provide the music. We agreed that his music and my words should not compete for the listener's attention, but be heard separately. On a later occasion I recorded at his house the traditional Irish melodies he had in mind for the subject. He played them on his pianola, and I listened to them again and again in Cleggan over the next few years, to infuse the words I was writing with their spirit. But I wanted the music to evoke the spirit of *both* sides in that conflict. Seán gave me only the tunes of the defeated. So I obtained LP recordings of Henry Purcell's music, with trumpets resounding in Westminster Abbey and a clavichord tinkling in a tower.

Martin Joyce told me what books of the period to read. On the Protestant side I used a 'true blue' eyewitness account by the Reverend George Storey, miscalled *An Impartial History of the Wars in Ireland*. Storey expresses what the English conquerors thought about the native Irish: that it would do us (Murphys etc.) good to be subjugated.

From local tradition I learned that one of my mother's ancestors, Robert Miller, then at Ballycushen Castle near Milford, had suborned a Spaniard of Irish descent, called O'Donnell of the Red Mouth, by keeping him and his thousand horsemen so drunk that they missed the battle. A Catholic stableboy had galloped off on O'Donnell's horse to warn the army of his treachery, but the horse had taken him astray. Long after the battle, at a gentlemen's club established by the Millers in Kilmaine – the one from which John Browne of the Neale was excluded for being the grandson of a papist – there was a toast drunk to the horse that had led the stable boy astray. Other legends from the Irish side I took to form in poetry an equation of the forces bent on each other's destruction on the battlefield.

A little research was to prove that my ancestors, like those of most people of Irish descent, had fought on opposite sides. If we could trace ourselves back eight or ten generations, each of us might learn of a thousand ancestors passing through their lives at that time, and we'd be humbled by the absurdity of pretentious ancestral claims, including mine. I learned that Patrick Sarsfield, the Norman Irish Catholic Jacobite hero who had sailed away in defeat to France, leading ten thousand Irish troops known as 'The Wild Geese' to win victories abroad, was my mother's distant uncle.

My stance was anti-triumphal, anti-militarist. As the horror of colonial warfare in Vietnam increased during the nineteen-sixties, the Irish situation in the sixteen-nineties seemed to connect more and more to the war that was finally won and lost at Aughrim: two great powers making use of foreign troops to fight battles on the soil of a poor distant country in the name of bitterly opposed beliefs. I was trying to examine my army heritage and my guilt in not having served in the war that was brought to an end by the bomb on Hiroshima on my 18th birthday. That heritage accounts for the coolness of tone and the demythologising ironies of the poem.

The poem grew slowly, because organically, from bits and pieces of my life and reading in Ireland between 1962 and 1967, not as a set-piece epic about a battle in the seventeenth century. As a renegade from a Protestant family that I loved, I wished the poem to unite my divided self in our divided country in a sequence faithful to the disunity of both.

My conclusion was that Ireland, united in a new united Europe, would be a happier country. But by the time I had finished the poem in October 1967, the earlier hope inspired by the cross-border meetings of Seán Lemass and Terence O'Neill had been destroyed in the North by the fury of Ian Paisley and the Protestant backlash; while nationalist feelings in the Republic were hardening, as the fiftieth anniversary celebrations of the Easter 1916 Rising culminated in the blowing up of Nelson's Pillar in front of the General Post Office.

From *The Kick: A Life Among Writers* (Lilliput Press e-book)

HISTORICAL NOTE

The battle of Aughrim (literally *horse ridge*) was fought on the evening of Sunday, July 12, 1691, about seventeen miles southwest of Athlone, almost in the centre of Ireland. It was a bloodier battle than the Boyne (1690), with four times as many casualties, and decisive in establishing Protestant rule over the whole of Ireland for the next two hundred years.

The Irish army was a native force, equipped by Louis XIV, and commanded by the French Marquis of St Ruth. Paid in brass, it fought in the name of King James II, an exile at St Germain, and in the Catholic interest.

The English army, aiding the planters in Ireland, was largely a force of foreigners, drawn from seven nations opposed to Louis, and commanded by a Dutch general, Baron Ginkel. Paid in silver and gold, it fought in the names of King William and Queen Mary (nephew and daughter of James), in the Protestant interest.

Since the previous summer, when James had been defeated by William at the Boyne, the Irish Jacobites continued to hold out in Connaught, led by the ageing viceroy, the Duke of Tyrconnel. Patrick Sarsfield, Governor of the western province, a major-general of the army, had saved the besieged town of Limerick by a daring raid on William's supplies in August. But though James had given Sarsfield the title Earl of Lucan, he had appointed a Frenchman Commander-in-Chief of the Irish army. St Ruth arrived at Limerick in May, lost Athlone by vanity and carelessness in June, and decided to stand at Aughrim on July 12 to restore his position and redeem his name.

Patrick Sarsfield disputed this hazardous strategy: his policy was to avoid risking the remnant of his nation in one great combat. St Ruth dismissed Sarsfield to the rear of the army, to command the reserve, and gave him no information about the battle. The Irish, strongly placed on the hill, held off the allied onslaught until St Ruth's decapitation by a cannonball. Then a traitor, Colonel Henry Luttrell, withdrew his cavalry from a vital pass. Sarsfield could do no more than cover the retreat to Limerick, where he signed the Treaty, and in October sailed to France with ten thousand troops (known as the Wild Geese) to join the Irish Brigade. Two years later, as a *Maréchal de camp*, he was mortally wounded at Landen in the French victory over William of Orange.

A note on the provenance of *The God Who Eats Corn*

One evening in May 1963, wearing canary yellow oilskins, I saw a well-dressed English couple looking forlorn on the quay at Cleggan, and I asked them if they wanted to sail on the *Ave Maria*.

'I'm Leonard Russell,' the man replied, 'and this is my wife, Dilys Powell.' She was a famous film critic and he the Chief Literary Editor of the London *Sunday Times*. They had heard of my boats, and seen copies of *Sailing to an Island* on display under a fishnet in the Pier Bar. After booking a trip to Inishbofin, they invited me to dine at Sweeney's Hotel in Oughterard the following night.

During dinner we talked about Lord Kemsley, their employer for many years. Russell told me that the first he knew about the sale of the *Sunday Times* was when Kemsley called him into his office, and showed him a cheque for £3,000,000 lying on his desk, a tactless exhibition, as Kemsley offered him no share. Russell asked for a photocopy of the cheque, which he pinned up in the lavatory used by guests at his house in London.

I told them that Lord Kemsley's son, Anthony Berry, had maimed and almost killed my younger sister in a motor accident caused by his drunkenness in the Bahamas in 1948, and that my father, out of courtesy to his guest at Government House, and deference to Lord Kemsley, had acted forgivingly and permitted Berry to leave the country and avoid prosecution.

Looking for work in London at the age of twenty-three, I had called on Lord Kemsley and asked to be given a chance to review poetry for the *Sunday Times*. He had told me bluntly to find a job as a reporter on a provincial newspaper and work my way up, but had not offered to introduce me to one of a dozen or more editors whose newspapers he owned. Otherwise, he had said, go and write a book which makes you famous, and then we'll come looking for you to write for us.

Leonard Russell, having listened with sympathy, said that if ever I cared to write a front page article for the literary section of the Sunday Times on a subject that might be of interest to the paper, he would pay £100. I thanked him, but explained that I would much rather write a poem than an article, however long or short. He responded encouragingly and said the serialisation of John Betjeman's *Summoned by Bells* had been a great success: no long poem had ever gained so many readers all at once. From the paper's point of view, he said, it would be a gimmick to commission a poem from a young poet who had recently launched his first book from Faber & Faber, but a gimmick he would like to try. The theme would have to be relevant.

A day or two later I showed him a draft of the first four lines of a poem about my father's life in retirement on a Southern Rhodesian farm. By the end of June he had given me a commission to write 'The God Who Eats Corn', stressing the point that it 'will have to be long enough to fill the front page of our weekly review section.' That meant about two hundred lines. The fee that I had asked – a return airline ticket to Rhodesia – would be paid if and when the poem was accepted.

To free myself for this work, I had to find a replacement skipper for one of the two hookers and a quiet room in which to write. Graham Tulloch, whose father had been a tea planter in Ceylon, lent me the use of a kitchen table, a hard chair and an iron bed with a horsehair mattress in a vast, vacant drawing room, without a carpet on the floor or curtains on the bay windows, in his decaying Victorian house. Graham farmed an inherited estate of mountain land that included High Island on which he grazed sheep.

In that room I worked for six or seven hours a day, between 11 and 6, while the hookers were at sea with tourists. The redolence of colonial power in decline at Shanbolard Hall was conducive to prolonged meditation on my father's life. He had been entertained in that room before he gained first class honours in classics at Trinity College, Dublin, and joined the Ceylon Civil Service in 1910, believing that Britain ruled her colonies for the benefit of the natives and set an example to the world. For this reason he expected the British Empire to last longer than the Roman, as we applied incorruptible justice rather than force to stay in power.

I had not been to Rhodesia since Christmas, 1959. Now I began to study the history and politics of central Africa. Four months later, Russell accepted the poem and sent me proofs, followed by a telegram saying, 'You can revise as freely as you wish in proof.'

Meanwhile, he had commissioned drawings by Leonard Rosoman, based on photographs of the farm and images in the poem. Both my parents had helped with advice on my father's life and the country's political history. By December the galleys had been corrected, and page proofs set up ready to print. The poem was scheduled to appear, filling the front page of the literary section of the *Sunday Times*, on the 29th December 1963. It was to mark the demise of the Central African Federation of Rhodesia and Nyasaland, and the independence of Zambia and Malawi, at the year's end. Faber informed the bookshops.

Before I had arrived in Rhodesia in time for Christmas, publication had been put off until the 5th January. But even then it didn't appear. Instead, a letter came from Russell's assistant, telling me, with no apology, that 'January 5 has been overtaken.' I felt crushed.

My parents were polite about the poem in their comments to me by mail, but face to face in the garden at Kiltullagh Farm that Christmas, my father told me what he really thought. He disliked my attitude, which had developed in ways he had never understood or approved, far from the colonies where he had lived for much of his life and nearly all of mine. Our long separations and the ways in which I had disappointed him had left scars.

He knew that the Central African Federation had been devised by white Rhodesians, led by Roy Welensky, as a means of transferring the wealth of the copperbelt from Northern to Southern Rhodesia, while supplying the south with docile unskilled labour from Nysasaland. But in 1957 he had been summoned out of retirement to act for three months as Governor-General, when Lord Llewellyn died in office; and his pride in the British colonial service would not allow him to tolerate what he perceived as criticism of its injustice by one of his sons, who owed his good education to that service. In a tone of injury, he said:

'I think the trouble with the poem is that you don't love Africa.'

He was right. I had perceived the poem as a portrait of a good man behaving as well as possible in a bad situation not of his making. Politically he supported Garfield Todd, leader of the only multiracial liberal party in Rhodesian politics. In this my father went against the grain of a massive majority of white settlers in that country, but won the respect of Africans. My poem had been an attempt to come closer to him with more understanding, from a distance of six thousand miles. I replied:

'The poem was written by someone who doesn't love Africa about a person who does, and perhaps the irony of this may increase the interest.'

I was sad to have failed to please my father by writing a poem in his honour. Worse still, I angered him so badly on that visit that he lost his temper one evening at dinner.

A barefoot black butler in a white uniform was timidly filling our glasses with South African wine. We were talking about the rapid decolonisation of Africa and what the results might be. My brother Edward had argued me into a corner, and provoked me to quote the report of a left-wing journalist, that only some thirty-eight white settlers were killed by the Mau Mau in Kenya, whereas the British army killed more than 10,000 Kikuyu in trying to suppress the rebellion.

This infuriated my father, who accused me of insulting the Colonial Service, to which he had devoted his life. He stood up to say this, deeply offended, much to my shame. Why could I not have kept my mouth shut, in spite of my brother's provocation?

Next day, on the verandah by the patio under hibiscus, beside a banana tree heavy with fruit, emerging from seclusion in his thatched rondavel study, where he had been reading Homer, he apologised in the natural way that he in his Church of Ireland Rectory youth had been taught, allowing me to feel forgiven and redeemed.

When I got back to London two weeks later, Russell explained that the Editor-in-Chief had cancelled 'The God Who Eats Corn,' because he wanted coverage of a surprise visit by the Pope to Jerusalem. Russell added that if there were to be a blood bath in Rhodesia, the Editor-in-Chief would want the poem to appear the following Sunday, otherwise he saw no hope of its inclusion in the *Sunday Times*. So he allowed it to be broadcast by the BBC and published by *The Listener* in London and the *Reporter* in New York.

My father could quote more Greek and Latin poetry by heart at seventy-five than I could quote English. While boarding at a grammar school for Protestant boys in Tipperary, he had not needed a threat of corporal punishment to study. He was brought up with the fear of hunger going back to his father's upbringing in a village schoolhouse in Carlow, and his grandfather Christopher Mulvany's memories of the great famine.

That was why he and my mother and my brother Edward, their farm manager, built a school on the farm to accommodate 250 African children from their own and neighbouring farms, who otherwise would have had no education. One of those children would become general manager of the Zimbabwean railways. Another would be a professor at a college in Texas where he would invite me to read my poetry in 1996.

From *The Kick: A Life Among Writers* (Lilliput Press e-book)

On the provenance of the High Island poems

My first impression of High Island had been formed in 1953 when Pat Concannon was teaching me how to sail a pookaun. Leaving Inishbofin harbour by the narrow channel between the Gun Rock and the Dog Fish Breaker, he had told me to head for High Island. But he'd never suggested landing there because it was five miles away and the landing on the island was impossible unless the sea was exceptionally calm – no pier to tie up at, no smooth sand for beaching a boat and no safe anchorage. Anyone trying to go ashore would have to jump from the boat to the rock and clamber up a cliff.

My first visit to High Island, or Ard Oilean in Irish, was on my father's last, sixty years after his first. With my mother, my younger sister Liz, and my daughter Emily, we managed to land on Sunday, 27th September 1964. The following Easter my father was buried in Clifden. My mother kept at her bedside until she died, nearly thirty years later, a photograph, taken by Liz, of my father sitting on the grass beside an ancient carved stone cross that greets pilgrims as they reach the top of the cliff above the landing cove on the southeast side. That was the origin of my interest in the island.

In the Pier Bar on the night of the 30th March 1969 I heard that the owner, Graham Tulloch, who had let me use his unfurnished drawing room for writing 'The God Who Eats Corn' in 1963, was planning to sell High Island because grazing sheep there had become unprofitable. I got excited at the thought of buying this inaccessible holy island, restoring the beehive cells and oratory of its derelict hermitage and preserving the place from destruction either by tourists or sheep.

I found a description of the island in a book written in 1684 by Roderic O'Flaherty:

> It is unaccessible but in calm settled weather, and so steep that it is hard after landing in it to climb to the top; where there is a well called Brian Boramy (King of Ireland) his well, and a standing water, on the brook whereof was a mill. There is extant a chappel and a large round wall, as also that kind of stone building called Cloghan. Therein yearly an eyrie of hawkes is found. Here St Fechin founded an abbey, as he did at Imay. It is also celebrated for the heremitical

retirement of Saint Gormgal, a very spiritual person, and of renouwned sanctity, who dyed the 5th of August, Anno 1017; and was there interred together with divers other holy hermits that lived with him.

The next morning I started negotiations with Graham, who wanted to sell two smaller islands with High Island (80 statute acres) because all three were on the same title deed. Quickly I found a couple willing to buy Friar and Malthooa, which, between them, had a safe harbour for a small boat in bad weather. Tony [White] rang at 6 p.m. from London to tell me that everyone at the cremation of Assia and Shura was speechless; he hadn't been able to say a word to Ted or Ted to him. Hearing about High Island, he urged me strongly to buy it. So I drove up to Shanbolard Hall and Graham accepted my offer. For little more than the University of Hull paid for my first stint of five weeks as the Compton Lecturer in Poetry I bought High Island, and the following day wrote this note:

Tuesday 1st April 1969 – Cleggan
Buying an island, even with the intention of creating a wild life sanctuary, is a predatory act among predators, much easier than writing a book. Once you become the owner, your view of the island alters: you turn possessive and protective. People regard you as a different person – a man who owns an island and therefore must be rich. But I know that High Island can never be possessed because it will always remain in the possession of the sea. Its virtue will grow from its contemplation not its use, from feelings and ideas evoked by its wild life and its end of the world terrain.

St Fechin, I knew, had founded monasteries in the seventh century at Fore in County Westmeath, Cong in County Mayo and on Omey Island (Imay). Now I was to learn that the hermitage on Ard Oilean, his last foundation before he died of the plague, was a cenobitic Laura where monks imposed on themselves extraordinary penances, and that Fechin 'used to set his wretched rib on the hard prison without raiment'.

According to John V. Kelleher of Harvard, St Gormgall was a noted *anmchara* – 'soul-friend' – of the High King Brian Boru, who was killed by a Dane at the Battle of Clontarf on Good Friday in 1014. The water in the well near the top of the hill on Ard Oilean was said to have turned into blood forever after the moment when the High King was slain. I'd noticed in 1964 that Brian Boru's well water was still dark red and undrinkable, but by 1969 it had turned black. When Pat Concannon had heard about this, he'd remarked, 'That must be on account of the trouble in the North.' Gormgall's name possibly meant 'dark stranger' but Kelleher thought 'blue valour' or 'blue-eyed foreigner' more likely, and the names of Gormgall's twelve fellow hermits, buried with him on the island, suggested that they had come from Clare, Brian's territory. With a scriptorium attached to the hermitage, Ard Oileán had been a literary as well as a religious centre. A poem was written about St Gormgall, but he didn't write poetry, which is what I was hoping the island would inspire.

My second stint (as the Compton Lecturer in Poetry) at Hull was happier than my first because I rented from the novelist Malcolm Bradbury a cottage situated beside an old church in a village called Lockington six miles from the University. My post merely required me to sit for a few hours a week in an office in the library where students showed me their work. Most days I had a stand-up lunch of beer and sandwiches with Philip Larkin, who used to drink two pints to my one. At my inaugural reading of *The Battle of Aughrim* he had switched off his hearing aid, fallen asleep and snored.

On the 14th May 1969 Ted (Hughes) rang to invite me over for the day to see his and the Brontë country, West Yorkshire. His mother had died and he was staying with his father at the Beacon above Heptonstall. Ted showed me a small redbrick end of terrace house in Mytholmroyd, where he had been born and spent his first eight years before the family moved to Mexborough. He took me through Hebden Bridge, where his mother and father had been born, telling me she was a Farrar, descended from the family of Nicholas Ferrar, one of the Little Gidding group in the 17th century. And he showed me Haworth.

His father could remember when four hundred men and women were employed at a textile mill in the narrow valley below his house, where nobody was working now. The workers had to walk in clogs ten miles across the moors from Burnley every morning and back at night, for most of the year in the dark. Ted's father used to swim in the warm dyed effluent of the mill, released promptly at 4.30 p.m. into the river.

After lunch Ted took me on foot down the hill below his father's house to see a place he had intended to buy with Assia six years ago, called the Manor Farm or Lumb Bank. The large stone house stood on a terrace cut into the hillside among fields walled with sandstone blackened by the smoke of extinct mills. Sixteen acres of land, Ted said, a house, a flat, two cottages, a barn, a walled garden, several fine beech trees and a folly. The slope felt vertiginous, like some of Ted's bird poems. We could see the rooftops of a town far below us to the east. The hill on the other side of the valley was wooded and equally precipitous.

As we were passing the gate, Ted told me that ten years ago a man who fancied this place had gone and knocked on the door and asked the old woman who lived there if she'd like to sell it for £2000, which she did. Hearing this, I suggested that he should do the same: go and knock on the door and ask the owners if they'd care to sell their house and land. Ted was looking for an alternative to Court Green. So we went together, and the man who answered our knocking said immediately that if anyone offered him £6000 cash, he'd be tempted.

On our walk back to the top of the hill, we were caught in a thunderstorm and our clothes were drenched. The lightning seemed to Ted a sign that he should buy the property, which in due course he did. Eventually he would employ Tony to convert it into a centre known as 'Arvon' to accommodate adult students for short courses in Creative Writing conducted by poets and novelists.

From Lumb Bank Ted took me to Heptonstall Church to see Sylvia's grave in a modern annexe to the old and overcrowded graveyard. Sylvia's grey headstone, simple and bold, carried a cryptic epigraph from the *Bhagavad Gita*, leaded into the granite: 'EVEN AMIDST FIERCE FLAMES THE GOLDEN LOTUS CAN BE PLANTED.'

Meanwhile, though he had driven with the children all the way from Devon the previous day, he had been working on his new selection of Shakespeare for Faber: scissoring out the passages he liked best, and pasting them into a book. He said that just before Assia's death he had been working on *Crow* and it had become so horrible he had put it aside. Of Assia herself he said, 'If I'd put a ring on her finger she'd still be alive.'

Two days later Ted paid a return visit to Lockington and stayed overnight. He offered to give some deer to High Island, if they would survive there. On Saturday, the 17th May, Philip Larkin and the young Scottish poet Douglas Dunn came to lunch. Philip wanted to take our photographs standing together in the graveyard, so he placed his camera, which had a time-switch, on a flat tombstone and joined the group himself before the camera clicked. While I was cooking our lunch, Douglas wanted to know how each of us got going on a poem. Philip replied that it was like knitting: you start with a certain number of stitches on a needle, having chosen a pattern that you have to complete. He also quoted 'the nightingale sings with her breast pressed against a thorn'. Not until many years later did I learn in Sri Lanka that Larkin's apparently flippant metaphor of knitting was rooted, though he may not have known this, in a single Sanskrit word with multiple meanings that included knitting, sewing, or the stitching together of words in poetry.

Being busy in the kitchen, I missed Douglas's answer to his own question and Ted's reply. But in Cleggan in 1966 he had told me how he sometimes got started on a poem. He'd sit on the edge of a bed and focus his mind on the coccyx or cuckoo bone at the base of his spine, blanking out all other thoughts, until he'd start to feel himself falling and falling as if from a great height through the bed and the floor and the ground, deeper and deeper into the underworld, till he'd fall into a wide-awake trance in which he'd assume the body of a bird, a beast, a fish, a tree or a stone. The poem from that depth might take off in ways he could never have consciously conceived. His fault, he said, was sometimes to bombard the poem with technique.

And I remember John McGahern once telling me, 'I look for the pain and when I find the pain I write.'

*

Needing a boat to reach High Island, I bought from Pete Burke, the son of Willie the Inishbofin boatwright, the decaying hull of the boat in which Pat Concannon and four others had survived the Cleggan Disaster. She had never been used since 1927, but kept in front of the Burkes' house above the shore of Bofin's East End harbour, as a reminder of the great storm. Pete had repaired her over the years to prevent her falling to pieces, never intending to put her again on the sea. When I asked him and Jim Cunnane, who had renovated the *Ave Maria* and built a punt for me in 1959, to build a pookaun on the model of Pete's relic, they agreed. We named the new boat the *Pateen*, after Pat Cloherty, who, sitting by his fire smoking his pipe, had recently died. The pookaun was to be powered by an outboard engine in addition to a dipping lugsail of tan terylene fastened to a gaff longer than the mast.

In August my mother and Emily, Chris and his wife, Marcelle, and their four children, Fiona, Anthony, Robert and Oona, with their Spanish Nanny, all stayed with me at the New Forge. Instead of buying a holy island that summer, Chris bought a derelict sixteenth-century Norman castle or tower house that he would reconstruct and use as a very large holiday home on the eastern shore of Lough Corrib near Headford. To prepare the roofless oratory on High Island for a Mass that we had arranged, Chris and his two sons and I went out in the *Pateen* on Saturday the 9th August. A note written two days later gave this account:

> Unscalable cliffs... groundswell resounding like a great deep-noted gong beaten inside the precipitous rock... fouled anchor... havenless shore... calm coves... slant slits in the mica schist rock... igneous formation... Chris was determined to rebuild the altar, using stones that were lying inside the church... the eastern gable had long ago collapsed into a mound of stones behind the altar... a few large stones had fallen off the top of the western gable, cluttering the doorway, which we cleared, thereby increasing its height... under the stones we found two stormpetrels' nests, each with a young bird opening its beak to be fed... two empty eggshells... our clearance to find a paved floor had violated the breeding of these shy birds... when a bird built a nest in St Kevin's hand while he was praying, he held the nest in his hand until the chickens had flown.

On the 13th August 1969 the sea having calmed enough for us to land on High Island, an eclectic group of Catholics (including my daughter, Emily, Mary Coyne and Margaret Day), Protestants (including my mother), and doubters like me came together at the hermitage to hear Mass – whether for summer entertainment, or in varying degrees of reverence for God, or the sea, or the island and all it contains of the past in the present. With sectarian conflict raging in the North, critics might say I had arranged the Mass to counter local objections to the island being bought by a Protestant, who sounded English, had divorced his wife, and might not believe in God. But I had multiple feelings about the island, and on this occasion felt euphoric.

A young priest, who had come with a boatload of people from Bofin, heard confessions on the grass, and Father Fergus from Claddaghduff agreed to use as much of the old Latin liturgy as he was allowed. Facing the priests at the altar inside the oratory, we knelt on clumps of thrift as soft as hassocks on a mound of stone that covered the hermits' graves. Two candles on the shelterless altar flickered but remained alight as the wind held its breath. Great black-back seagulls clanged in protest without remission. The declining sun was turning the ocean into a lake of fire. Emily, standing behind the two priests, read from the Wisdom of Solomon about those who have not set their hearts on riches, who could have transgressed but have not transgressed. She held the cadence in the air as gracefully as a bird instinctively timing the beat of its wings. In twos and threes, nine communicants came and knelt on the stones near the altar, and one by one leaned forward so that the hand of the priest could reach their tongues with the host.

> Wednesday 3 September 1969, High Island
> I am alone on Ard Oilean for the first time… at the top of the cove, looking down on the landing-place… the pookaun moored, the sea calm, ebb tide, afternoon… now I have two penitential tasks to complete… the purification of the well, and the restoration of the stone incised with a peculiar cross whose arms are like horns, the stone I took from beside the well two years ago and kept in my garden… it was heavy to carry up the cliff on my own today… now I have roped it, and I'll try to drag it up the hill to the well without breaking it…

At the time I wrote that note I could see clearly all the islands and the mainland between Achill Island and Slyne Head. I began my task by dragging the stone cross with a harness of halyards over long coarse grass pitted with rabbit burrows, panting, halting, straining uphill, and along the cliff edge, all the way to the well. First, I moved the stones that shepherds had put round the well to prevent sheep drowning there – the skull of a dead sheep lay in the top scraw at the entrance – then shook a handful of lime on the putrid water, bailed it with a bucket, and finally scooped up in my hands a silt of black slime containing the bowl of a clay pipe, a few copper pennies and a silver florin, buttons and a cotton reel. Next, I dug an outlet through the bog to keep the water fresh by flowing. For more than a thousand years the peat had risen around the well, causing the water to stagnate.

Four hours I worked, my hands blistering, and had a great reward. Deep in the bog, but only a step from the well, the spade struck a stone, which I dug out carefully. When my nails had scraped off the roots that clung to it, I recognised the broken top of a small cross with roughly weathered arms that stretched as far as the stone would allow the carver to shape them. It was delicately engraved on one side with a Greek cross jewelled with four embossed circles in the angles of the arms. Probably more than a thousand years old, and buried for much of that time.

I'd been warned in Cleggan not to tamper with Brian Boru's well because it was sacred, but now I was proud of my work, feeling that the cross was a reward, a sign that my attempt to purify the water had not violated the well's holiness. At that moment I struck my back against a stone sharply, and cried out with pain. It was then that I first noticed a fog bank looming on the horizon. As it reached and drenched the island in mist, I planted the stone cross firmly in the ground beside the well, my task completed. Aching, parched and exhausted, I walked down to the cliff above the landing, paused to rest on a clump of thrift among quartz rocks surrounded by sea asters. From there I could see the pookaun securely moored in the mouth of the cove, and drank the last drop of tea from a thermos.

Then I prayed, or almost, at the cross where my father had sat on the turf to be photographed the summer before he died; and climbed down the steep rock to the landing place, launched the Zodiac dinghy, got my gear aboard. As I was standing in the pookaun, wondering should I wait for the fog to clear, or haul up the anchor and risk being wrecked on a submerged rock, capsized by a breaker, or carried out to sea by a two-knot current in the sound between High Island and Friar, I heard a voice that pierced me. It was very clear, high and beautiful, crying and exulting from the darkness of a cove. I presumed it came from a seal, but it sounded like a solo in a requiem or a clarinet in a concerto of the sea. Combining joy with lamentation in a falling atonal cry, it seemed to emanate from the heart of all creatures and go beyond the utmost human grief to reach the music of the spheres. Mermaid, Banshee and Siren crossed my mind. It left me shaken, enthralled.

As the song ended, a lobster boat, with an aerial in the shape of a cross on the masthead, appeared out of the mist. Salvation? Not at all. She turned, and, without a wave of greeting or goodbye from the crew, headed out of sight like a phantom ship. Then the voice cried out again, and though the fog had thickened, the second song removed my fear, leaving calm of mind – or was it light-headedness? – to face whatever might occur.

I started the engine and put to sea, keeping close to the shore, trying to avoid the cork-buoyed ropes of lobster pots. The fog signal boomed from Slyne Head. When I lost sight of High Island, I couldn't see Friar, and when I found Friar I had to change course and steer south around it, then east.

The smallest rocky island loomed through the fog as large as a mountain, but the sea was flat calm. With no land in sight, using a small pocket compass to avoid Crow's Rock, I was looking down in the deep water when – too quickly for me to change course – the tip of a rock appeared under the keel as we passed. The song that had lured me to my drowning had helped me to survive.

Just before nightfall I recognised houses near the point of Ganogues, and from there I could keep close to shore all the way to Aughrus. I was met on the pier by a stray dog.

Over the years I heard many versions of the legend that a poor young woman, who lived with her husband in a sod-hut at Aughrusmore long ago, had been landed by her husband and his mate on High Island, either to pick carrageen, dillisk and sloke for food, or grass for a cow on the mainland, or to sheer sheep for a farmer, while the men went fishing in a curragh. Her time was due for giving birth to her first child. A storm blew up from the west and the men were barely able to save their lives when the curragh was swept back to Aughrusmore. For three days the woman was left alone on the island without food or shelter except for one clochan or beehive cell at the hermitage. When the sea calmed, the men rowed out expecting to have to bring back her remains, and were amazed to see her climbing down the cliff with a baby in her arms.

According to an account from that child's great-grandson, John Joyce of Inishbofin, when he was very old, the woman had taken refuge in the clochan, 'And as she started to give birth in the night a lamp was brought by a mysterious hand that gave her all the help she needed, and when the child was born the mysterious hand gave her a little garb to put on the child. People who had sick children used to come from all over Connemara to get a portion of the mysterious garb.'

From *The Kick: A Life Among Writers* (Lilliput Press e-book)

Critique of 'Pat Cloherty's Version of *The Maisie*'

by BERNARD O'DONOGHUE

Everyone knows, but still remarks as if it were something new, that Words-worth's ambition to write 'in the language of a man speaking to men' was apparently not successful. The ideal of writing in an unliterary language, in a real vernacular, seems to be rechampioned in every generation. It is invoked both for and against existing writing. In his *De Vulgari Eloquentia* in about 1290, Dante argued (in Latin) the case for composing the *Divine Comedy* in the Italian vernacular rather than in learned Latin. As an example of the unvernacular, Macaulay grumbled in 1831 about the language of Dr Johnson: 'All his books are written in a learned language, in a language which nobody hears from his mother or his nurse, a language in which nobody ever quarrels, or drives bargains, or makes love, a language in which nobody ever thinks'. The obligation implied in all this is one which weighs particularly heavily on poets; in an Irish context, Yeats stated it most dramatically and memorably in his late 'General Introduction for my Work': 'I tried to make the language of poetry coincide with that of passionate, normal speech. I wanted to write in whatever language comes most naturally when we soliloquise... upon the events of our own lives... I sometimes compare myself with the mad old slum women I hear denouncing and remembering; "How dare you", I heard one say of some imaginary suitor, "and you without health or a home".'[1] Nevertheless, Yeats concludes that he 'must seek, not as Wordsworth thought, words in common use, but a powerful and passionate syntax.' (521-2)

Wordsworth was far from unique in failing to remain true to his ideal. There are far more striking failures: T.S. Eliot's embarrassing vernacular at the end of the 'Game of Chess' section of *The Waste Land*, for example; or even worse, Yeats's own 'Ballad of Moll Magee':

> Come round me, little childer;
> There, don't fling stones at me.

It is a lot easier to illustrate such failures than the vernacular successes

---

1. W.B. Yeats, *Essays and Introductions* (London: Macmillan, 1961), 521. Original essay 1937.

(amongst the latter are perhaps some of Child's Ballads, Burns, John Clare, Augusta Gregory, Hugh MacDiarmid). The poem I want to consider here, Richard Murphy's 'Pat Cloherty's Version of *The Maisie*'[2] seems to me a striking, and at first glance surprising, success in this area. The success is surprising for a variety of reasons: the principal one that Murphy, an Oxford-educated Anglo-Irishman, might not be expected to be the most obvious reproducer of a local language, as he readily concedes himself. He discusses his heritage at various points in his lively and revealing memoir *The Kick*, noting in Connemara his 'precarious footing as an outsider, a divorced Protestant with a British accent in a village then under the sway of a priest, who had no liking for me or for Protestants or for Brits'.[3]

The context and prehistory in Murphy's writing of the vernacular success of the 'Maisie' poem is significant. Although some of his Anglo-Irish fore-bears came from Mayo, there is no doubt that literary predecessors were at least as influential as family ones on his decision to follow the sleepy resolve of Gabriel Conroy at the end of 'The Dead', 'to set out on his journey westward'. Obvious influences are Synge's living on Inis Meáin and Yeats's taking up residence in Thoor Ballylee. Murphy had made the remarkable decision in the 1950s to settle down in Cleggan for the summer months and to operate first one (bought in the hot summer of 1959) and later two Galway hookers to ferry visitors over to Inishbofin. And in 1969, he bought High Island as an even more remarkable west-locating venture.

In poetic terms, Murphy's journey westward was a resounding success from the first. His highly successful first book *Sailing to an Island*[4] made much of its impact in the three sailing poems comprising Part One. The title-poem which opens the volume is decidedly English-poetic in style.:

> Encased in a mirage, steam on the water
> Loosely we coast where hideous rocks jag,
> An acropolis of cormorants, an extinct
> Volcano where spiders spin, a purgatory
> Guarded by hags and bristled with breakers. [19; *SI*, 13]

2. See pp.113-15 of this edition. Richard Murphy, *High Island* (London: Faber & Faber, 1974), 25-27. Later references in the text as *HI*.

3 Richard Murphy, *The Kick: A Memoir* (London: Granta Books, 2002), 227. [Reissued by Lilliput Press as an ebook, 2013.]

4. Richard Murphy, *Sailing to an Island* (London: Faber & Faber, 1963). Later references in the text as *SI*.

The elaborate diction describes sailors as 'those who must earn their living / On the ribald face of a mad mistress', and recalls that this boat 'belched its crew / Dead on the shingle in the Cleggan disaster'. The second poem, 'The Last Galway Hooker', celebrates Murphy's boat, the *Ave Maria*, which an introductory note tells us was built in Galway in 1922 (Murphy plied it until 1964 when he sold both his boats). The headnote concludes with a significant 'Metrical Note': 'The typical line has four stresses (though not of equal emphasis) which fall usually into two groups of two stresses each. The opening lines set the pattern as follows, with the words that contain the stresses in italics, and the caesura (which is long) marked with an apostrophe:

> Where the *Corrib* river ' chops through the *Claddagh*
> To *sink* in the tide-race ' its *rattling chain*
> The *boatwright's hammer* ' *chipped* across the *water* ' [36; *SI*, 16]

Despite the poem's subject, the metrical form Murphy sets out here is familiar as the standard way of representing the stress-pattern traditions of English, from Old English to Hopkins and Auden. The poem also of course is not unmindful of one of the great translations from Irish, 'Anach Cuan' by Pádraig de Brún, a version of Antoine Raftery's lyrical lament in Irish about the drowning of nineteen people on the river Corrib near Galway in 1828, almost exactly a century earlier.[5] This may indeed constitute a further connexion with Yeats who was very aware of Raftery's life in the area around Gort, Co. Galway, commemorated in the poem 'The Tower' and elsewhere.

The last of the poems of Part 1 of *Sailing to an Island*, 'The Cleggan Disaster', returns more extensively to the story mentioned in the title-poem. The story was told to Murphy by Pat Concannon who is the central figure in the poem, recounting his eight-hour struggle for survival in a rowing boat during a famous storm in October 1927. The poem is an unquestionable and original success, but still in a mode familiar from the traditions of English poetry. It is not a negative criticism to say that the poem, like its two predecessors, thrives on poetic devices; indeed they are a contribution to its success: 'not a flicker of a fish', 'the lightning flaked / in willow cascades', 'the wind began to play, like country fiddlers / In a crowded

---

5. 'Eanach Dhúin': noted in *The Connaught Journal* of Thursday 4 September, 1828.

room'. And the poem concludes with a lyrical series of elegiac stanzas of *ubi sunt* in a different measure: 'Where are the red-haired women / Chattering along the piers / Who gutted millions of mackerel?' The subject-matter of all this is Irish and local, but the language and the poetics belong to English. 'The Cleggan Disaster' has major importance as a long narrative poem of compelling excitement and animation that it is not easy to find equalled in its era. But, reading through it, although there are vernacular touches like 'The oarsmen were calling Concannon to let go, / Take it easy for a while', or the more self-conscious 'Darker it's getting' (51, 50; *SI*, 26, 24), the prevailing language is a kind of standard English narrative, very successfully employed. Though Murphy had received the story of the disaster from Concannon himself, the poem adapts his voice to the literary eloquence of the English tradition.

However, when we come to 'Pat Cloherty's Version of *The Maisie*' ten years later, although it is thematically continuous from these three poems, its language and poetic manner are totally different. It represents a major innovation, despite the familiarity of its subject within Murphy's corpus. Murphy's circumstances in the interval between the two books had changed, by making his westward move more decisive. When he bought High Island in 1969, he built an austere cottage on it that could be inhabited for the summer months, in the footsteps of the medieval monks who had settled more permanently along the Atlantic coast on such islands, including this one. Like 'The Cleggan Disaster', the poem draws on a received narrative; but it is clear from the start that it will draw on it much more directly. The story this time comes from Pat Cloherty, another Cleggan friend of Murphy's, recounting not his own experience but the loss of a hooker called *The Maisie* in 1884, as described in local narrative. There is an immediate irony here: the substance of the poem is Cloherty's telling – his 'version' – as the title indicates, which is as prominent as the events it is relating. The irony is that the voice and personality of the teller are more evident here in this retailed narrative than in Concannon's description of his own experience. In a 'version', the language is foregrounded, in a way that the rather Conradian narrative of the Cleggan poem did not need to be. And, formally structured though the poem is, Murphy purports to present the language unmediated.

The poem begins with a classic instance of the art concealing art which emerges as the distinguishing hallmark of the poem:

I've no tooth to sing you the song
    Tierney made at the time
        but I'll tell the truth   [113; *HI*, 25]

There is plenty of dialectal strangeness here: is 'tooth' used in this way, in Irish-English or in Irish, to mean 'note' (as in 'he hasn't a note in his head')? It doesn't matter; the usage serves its purpose at once. We might note, on closer examination, how 'tooth' and 'truth', though they are two lines apart, are a kind of slant rhyme of the kind that Austin Clarke brought into English from Irish in his 'Celtic-Romanesque' mode. This kind of stylistic feature recurs in the poem: for example in the echoing 'ei' vowels ('Clare', Cahir', 'mainsail', 'foresail') in

She passed Clare and she came to Cahir
    two reefs tied in the mainsail
        she bore a foresail but no jib   [113; *HI*, 26]

As the storyline develops, it is clear that here too we have moved from the world of Joseph Conrad in 'The Cleggan Disaster' to that of J.M. Synge in *Riders to the Sea* and *The Aran Islands*:

The men were two stepbrothers
    drownings in the family
        and all through the family   [113; *HI*, 25]

Everything in the poem continues in an Irish tradition, of language and poetics as well as subject matter. Some of the effects of language are taken directly from the speaker's mouth with no recasting at all, it seems (like 'I've no tooth'):

    hugging it   hugging it   O my dear

And it blew and blew hard and blew hard [113-14; *HI*, 26]

But the crucial thing to note here is that, despite the affinities with earlier Irish literary traditions and the claimed closeness of the language to the speech of Cloherty, the poem is extraordinarily original in form. The three-line stanza, with its progressive indentations, achieves a plainness of great effectiveness, most notably at the poem's end which reads like a cemetery inscription:

277

>   Kerrigan's wife was brought from Cross
>   home to Inishbofin
>   and she's buried there

Upon examination, the devices by which Murphy achieves this plainness are sustained through the poem, and they are often effects well established in handbooks of poetics and even classical rhetoric: repetition ('it blew and blew hard and blew hard'); breach of rules of punctuation – apart from capital letters at the opening of each stanza and the caesural gaps as in the 'hugging it' line, there is no mark of punctuation in the poem; phonetic echoing in the occasional rhymes and half-rhymes ('found' / 'Sound'; 'Pier' / 'there'); and so on. In summary, the poem's impression of plainness is achieved in a form of highly worked intricacy, as plainness always is: the trick of seeming 'clear / as the bleb of the icicle', as Seamus Heaney memorably phrased it at the end of 'North'. Of course Wordsworth did sometimes achieve the impression of a man speaking to men ('If Lucy should be dead!'), but that is as much of a rhetorical structure as anything else.

'Pat Cloherty's Version of *The Maisie*' is all the more effective for being distinctive within *High Island*, both in subject and form. The three sailing poems in *Sailing to an Island* constitute a compelling block of narrative; this poem in *High Island* stands out like a rock in the sea. Formally too it is unique; the recurring themes of the volume are entirely in keeping with the poem's setting (travellers, birds, history, buildings, all located in the west of Ireland), but the language of the rest of the poems is invariably standard. It is more spare than the language of the earlier book, but Pat Cloherty's voice is the only element of dialect here. No doubt Murphy has taken over many of the words and phrases of the original narrative, in the time-honoured way of oral tradition.[6] In that tradition, many effects are not to be assigned to the characteristics of a particular voice; the repeated phrases – 'the sea claimed him', 'he's buried there', 'it blew hard' – are classic oral formulas, open to mild modification. Here these formulas are mixed with more particular cultural and linguistic details: 'missing Mass to

---

6. Murphy has shown me a typescript of the recording he made of Pateen Cloherty's narrative in 1968. Much of the detail of the language of the poem is drawn directly from the narrative, including some of the poetics, such as the division of the line into triads. But looking at the source has only enhanced my admiration for the fidelity and originality of the poem's language.

catch the tide', 'like a person'd be in prayer', the grammatical irregularity of the double negative 'the sea never came in / near that mark no more'.[7] This plain narrative tapestry is indeed a complex of intricate threads.

So what is the place of this poem (which I believe to be a masterpiece) in the modern Irish – and English – poetic tradition? What kind of enablement might it offer to later poets? Richard Murphy's place in the narrative of both traditions is now seriously underrated; when *High Island* was published, only Hughes, Plath and Larkin had a comparable standing amongst poets published in London. In the poetics of the Irish tradition in particular he is as important a mediator from Yeats to the modern writers as anyone – comparable to MacNeice or Kavanagh. In this way he belongs to the high tradition of modern Irish poetry in English. But the Maisie poem does something else perhaps even more remarkable. It is written in an oral tradition; but that tradition did not exist; it had to invent the world that it belongs to. Other poets share details with it; Heaney's 'fother' at the start of *Wintering Out*, or his etymological explorations in 'Broagh' are distinguished relations; so are Montague's etymological usages in *The Rough Field*. But Heaney and most other writers hold back from full-scale oral telling (even restoring standard English forms, as Heaney notes himself in relation to John Clare). By creating an oral poetic world for Pat Cloherty's version to belong to, Murphy really is doing something genuinely vernacular. We might want to propose 'synthetic Scots' as a parallel; but that language, to my ear, for all its poetic excellence lacks the impression of local authenticity that Murphy achieves here. It is surprising I think how few Irish poets have followed his lead in attempting to write a 'version': the new poetic genre that this poem creates. But perhaps this is because such an authentic vernacular is very hard to construct. T.S. Eliot said in praise of Yeats that sensibility changes from generation to generation, but expression is changed only by a writer of genius: 'in becoming more Irish, not in subject-matter but in expression, he became at the same time universal'.[8] Murphy's creation of a poetic language for this narrative is another instance of this principle.

7. It strikes me as interesting, incidentally, that an important short poem in the volume is called 'Double Negative'.

8. T.S. Eliot, 'Yeats' – the first Annual Yeats Lecture, delivered to the Friends of the Irish Academy at the Abbey Theatre, Dublin, 30 June 1940.

INDEX

Index of titles and first lines

(Titles and sub-titles are shown in italics, first lines in roman type.)

285

RICHARD MURPHY

Born in 1927 at Milford, near Kilmaine, County Mayo,
Richard Murphy spent part of his childhood in Ceylon,
where his father was the last British Mayor of Colombo.
From the age of eight, he attended boarding schools in
Ireland and England, winning a scholarship to Oxford
at seventeen. After years of displacement, marriage and
divorce, he returned to Inishbofin in 1959 and settled
for twenty years at Cleggan, writing there and on Omey
and alone on High Island. He moved to Dublin in 1980,
detaching himself from the beloved country of his past
the better to reach it in poetry. Living since 2007 near
Kandy in Sri Lanka, he finished this book while building
a clay-tiled Octagon on a hill-top, for writing, meditation
and yoga.